Great Barrington Books

Bringing the old and new together
in the spirit of W. E. B. Du Bois

∿ An imprint edited by Charles Lemert ∿

Titles Available

Keeping Good Time: Reflections on Knowledge, Power, and People
by Avery F. Gordon (2004)

Going Down for Air: A Memoir in Search of a Subject
by Derek Sayer (2004)

The Souls of Black Folk,
100th Anniversary Edition
by W. E. B. Du Bois, with commentaries by Manning Marable, Charles Lemert,
and Cheryl Townsend Gilkes (2004)

Sociology After the Crisis, Updated Edition
by Charles Lemert (2004)

Subject to Ourselves
by Anthony Elliot (2004)

The Protestant Ethic Turns 100:
Essays on the Centenary of the Weber Thesis
edited by William H. Swatos, Jr., and Lutz Kaelber (2005)

Postmodernism Is Not What You Think
by Charles Lemert (2005)

Discourses on Liberation: An Anatomy of Critical Theory
by Kyung-Man Kim (2005)

Seeing Sociologically: The Routine Grounds of Social Action
by Harold Garfinkel, edited and introduced by Anne Warfield Rawls (2005)

The Souls of W. E. B. Du Bois
by Alford A. Young, Jr., Manning Marable, Elizabeth Higginbotham, Charles
Lemert, and Jerry G. Watts (2006)

Radical Nomad: C. Wright Mills and His Times
by Tom Hayden with Contemporary Reflections by Stanley Aronowitz, Richard
Flacks, and Charles Lemert (2006)

Critique for What? Cultural Studies, American Studies, Left Studies
by Joel Pfister (2006)

Everyday Life and the State
by Peter Bratsis (2006)

Forthcoming
Thinking the Unthinkable:
An Introduction to Social Theories
by Charles Lemert

Everyday Life and the State

Peter Bratsis

Paradigm Publishers
Boulder • London

Copyright © 2006 Paradigm Publishers

Published in the United States by Paradigm Publishers, 3360 Mitchell Lane Suite E, Boulder, CO 80301 USA.

Paradigm Publishers is the trade name of Birkenkamp & Company, LLC, Dean Birkenkamp, President and Publisher.

Library of Congress Cataloging-in-Publication Data

Bratsis, Peter.
   Everyday life and the state / Peter Bratsis.
      p. cm.
   Includes bibliographical references and index.
   ISBN-13: 978-1-59451-218-6 (hc : alk. paper)
   ISBN-10: 1-59451-218-3 (hc : alk. paper)
   1. Political sociology. 2. State, The. I. Title.
   JA76.B724 2006
   306.2—dc22

                                                      2006012369

Printed and bound in the United States of America on acid free paper that meets the standards of the American National Standard for Permanence of Paper for Printed Library Materials.

10 09 08 07 06   1 2 3 4 5

The theory of the capitalist State cannot be isolated from the history of its constitution and reproduction.
—Nicos Poulantzas, *State, Power, Socialism*

Contents

Acknowledgments

This book is the outcome of my PhD dissertation. I would like to thank all those who were kind enough to discuss, read, and advise me on its content. Lenny Markovitz has been a very treasured teacher and advisor. At all times, he has given me insightful and valuable advice. His encouragement and belief in the value of this project have helped me through the periods of doubt that accompany research and writing. Finally, to whatever degree the ideas and words that follow are clear and free from jargon, it is largely due to Lenny's influence. Stanley Aronowitz has introduced me to many of the concepts and texts discussed in the following pages, and without him it would have been impossible to conceive and execute this project. He has been a valued and trusted mentor and has taught me the difference between scholarship and intellectual creation. Frances Fox Piven has not only provided me with thoughtful comments and critiques, but her intellectual honesty and political relevance have served as models that I hope to be able to follow. John Bowman introduced me to much of the literature within political economy and state theory, and this book has greatly benefited from his critical and rigorous readings. The chapter on political corruption has been greatly aided by many discussions with Constantine Tsoukalas, who first convinced me of the merits of studying corruption. My knowledge of state theory was greatly advanced by my many discussions and debates with Ralph Miliband, one of the most kind and generous people I have known. Andreas Karras has been charitable enough to read the manuscript multiple times, and his advice and suggestions have been crucial to this project and those that led up to it. Similarly, Eleni Natsiopoulou has read the manuscript multiple times, and her critiques, challenges, and support have made this book much better than it could have been without her. I would also like to thank W. Ofuatey-Kodjoe for his support of my research and for helping secure the institutional freedom to pursue it. My collaborations and discussions with José Eisenberg were very important to the conception of this project and many of the questions contained within it. Nicos Alexiou, João Feres, Heather Gautney, Bruno Gulli, David Harvey, Bob Jessop, Andreas Kalyvas, Andrew Lawrence, Marena Lobosco, Roland Marden, Randy Martin, Mike Menser, Leo Panitch, Michael Pelias, and Yannis Stavrakakis have read all or parts of this work and have given me valuable comments and advice. I wish to thank the Center for Byzantine and Modern Greek Studies of Queens College for a grant and logistical support that enabled my study of the Greek Americans. Finally, I wish to thank Dean Birkenkamp and the editorial and production staff at Paradigm Publishers for all their work and patience.

Some chapters have been previously published elsewhere. A slightly earlier version of Chapter 1 was published in Stanley Aronowitz and Peter Bratsis, eds., *Paradigm Lost: State Theory Reconsidered* (University of Minnesota Press, 2002); most of Chapter 3 first appeared in *Social Text* 77 (2003); and an early version of Chapter 4 appeared in *Found Object* 8 (2000).

Introduction:
Don't Take It Literally

> Quite generally, the familiar, just because it is familiar, is not
> cognitively understood. The commonest way in which we de-
> ceive either ourselves or others about understanding is by as-
> suming something as familiar, and accepting it on that ac-
> count.
> —G.W.F. Hegel, *Phenomenology of Spirit*

During the war in Kosovo, the Greek chapter of *Doctors Without Borders*
(*Medecins Sans Frontieres*) was expelled for sending a team of doctors to Ser-
bia.[1] This move took many by surprise, emphasizing the folly of taking the name
of the organization literally as well as demonstrating the widespread tendency,
even among those on the left, to do so. Moreover, the fact that *Doctors Without
Borders* is organized into *national* chapters is in itself a clear sign of the falsity
of the claim of being borderless. Along similar lines, "set it and forget it" is the
advertising slogan for a popular home rotisserie that is sold through late-night
infomercials. It seems, however, that "forgetting it" is not advisable. A large
warning is pasted to the front of each machine that, referring to the slogan, ad-
vises customers not to "take it literally." Following the directive of the slogan
would eventually lead to an overcooked kitchen.

The disconnect evident between rhetoric and actuality in the above examples is obvious. These cursory examples also highlight a key epistemological
hurdle for social science, going beyond appearances and the familiar in order to
achieve a more rigorous and objective understanding of social reality. The pitfalls of taking things literally are not limited to the arena of slogans and public
relations. A key goal of the present work is to overcome similar disconnects
within the social scientific literature on the state.

Foremost in this regard, and most surprisingly, there has long been a
disconnect within the Marxist literature on the state. Those contributions that
have come to be known as state theory, despite the name, have not been a theory
of the state.[2] State theory, rather than being an attempt to explain the state, has

---

[1] They have since been reinstated.

[2] Adam Przeworski has noted this point, "Much of what passes for Marxist theory of the
state is in fact a state theory of capitalist reproduction, that is, a theory that explains the

1

mostly been concerned with theorizing the functions of the state and its roles within the processes of capitalist exploitation. According to Bob Jessop:

> Much Marxist theorizing has focused on the state's functions for capital; the better sort has examined its form and shown how this problematizes these functions; none has put the very existence of the state in question. (Jessop 1990, xi)

Phrased another way, Marxism has taken the state literally and has thus failed to interrogate the deeper truths that the self-presentation of the state may be covering over. Just as a great many were taken in by the false image of saintly doctors who would stop at no border in order to provide medical care, so too many have been bamboozled by the blinding familiarity of the state.

A second moment of disconnect within the ever-expanding literature on the state has been a lack of analysis regarding the state itself. Many recent contributions that are nominally works *of* political or state theory are in fact works *on* state/political theory.[3] The growing tendency has been to discuss the theories and not the state. Mark J. Smith puts things very clearly in the beginning of his *Rethinking State Theory*: "Many books have been written about *"the state"*; this is not one of them (Smith 2000, 1)." There is no doubt that critical reviews of the literature serve important functions and are a necessary component of any rigorous analytical work.[4] The problem is when the concepts and theorists become the focus rather than a means toward the ends of concrete analysis. For example, Jens Bartelson's *The Critique of the State* is by most measures a serious, imaginative, and subversive review of contemporary political theory. It is also a book that shares a central argument with the present work: that social scientific theory tends to take the state as a given, that contemporary political theory is, in Bartelson's terms, "statist." Unfortunately, however good Bartelson's reading of texts may be, he is reluctant to link the theoretical tendencies he discusses with the state itself or any other concrete social phenomena:

> My claim is therefore that an analysis of the presupposed presence of the state in political discourse can, and indeed must, be undertaken while remaining agnostic about the actual claims

---

reproduction of capitalist relations in terms of the role played by the state" (Przeworski 1985, 224).

[3] This tendency can be seen as a reflection of a broader trend within political theory where texts (not social/political phenomena) have come to be considered the key objects of analysis.

[4] Moreover, many works of review, from various essays by Bob Jessop and David Held (Jessop 1990; Held 1989), to Martin Carnoy's seminal *The State and Political Theory* (1984), to Clyde Barrow's more recent overview (1993), have served to introduce a great many scholars to the questions and concepts of state theories and have also framed the reception of these theories.

about the ontological status of the state advanced within a given discourse. (Bartelson 2001, 6)

It should be pointed out that by "political discourse" Bartelson is referring to contemporary political theory; theorists like David Easton and Giorgio Agamben, among others. He attempts to show how the idea of the state is foundational to the very emergence of political science as a discipline and how even those theories that try to discard the concept of the state continue to presuppose it. Of what utility is such an analysis if it, according to Bartelson's own claim, says nothing about the existence of the state? For Bartelson the key problem is that by presupposing the state, current "political discourse" does not allow for a non-statist imagining of politics and further reproduces the key presuppositions of the state, the state/society divide, and/or the national polity. It is as if Easton, Ralph Miliband, Claus Offe, and so on were the sources of what social actors perceive as reality; as if the idea of the state was the product of academic scholars and their debates. It is here that we see the kinds of idealism and scholasticism that even the most critical and thoughtful of projects can fall into when the emphasis is on texts and concepts at the exclusion of the analysis of actual social practices.

    This book is, in large part, a response to these tendencies within political theory that either take the state literally, as an ontological given, or reduce it to the "literary"; treat it as merely a taxonomical category and discuss it as if it were an academic definition. As much progress as contemporary political and social thought have made on a great many issues, it is a telling failure that we have not advanced very far from Thomas Hobbes's positions regarding the production of the state. This book is an attempt to bring the question of the state's ontology to the fore of political theory and to redirect its gaze away from the textual and scholastic.

Situating the Arguments

In Chapter 1, Marxist state theory will be used to frame the remainder of this book. This reflects the developmental trajectory of the problematic presented here. It is through engagements with and within Marxist theory that the key questions being posed here came about. This does not imply, however, that the relevance of the arguments is exclusive to Marxism. Obviously, the failure to take the state itself as something to be explained is not particular to Marxism (as Bartelson's book very well documents). Indeed, it is that "even" Marxist state theory has tended to assume the state since it may have been expected that, of all social scientific traditions, state theory should have been the least likely to take the state as a given. As such, the relevance of the break that I am attempting here extends well beyond the domains of Marxist state theory. This is true in terms of academic literatures and also in terms of pertinent research questions and social analyses.

Looking back upon the twentieth century, we see that the two greatest moments in the development of the theory of the state were very much tied to pressing pragmatic political questions and were engaged in broad topics of social importance. Most notably, there is a twenty-year span in which Lenin, Rosa Luxemburg, Max Weber, Antonio Gramsci, Carl Schmitt, and various Frankfurt school theorists (such as Franz Neumann and Otto Kirchheimer) produced a very deep and foundational set of insights on the state. A generation later, C. Wright Mills, Louis Althusser, Ralph Miliband, Henri Lefebvre, Nicos Poulantzas, James O'Conner, Claus Offe, Fred Block, and others offered another round of critical reflection on the state. In both cases, even the most esoteric of theories were keenly engaged with the political turmoil and possibilities of the times.

It may be true that state theory today is somewhat less urgent and illustrious. There are, however, emerging tendencies and extremely pertinent analytical tasks that have come to characterize a new chapter in the study of the state. When Bob Jessop (1990, 7) made the observation, cited previously, that state theory did not question the existence of the state, he pointed to two examples of theorists who had gone beyond the tendency to take the state as a given, Hans Kelsen (1945) and Philip Abrams (1988). Slightly over a decade later, Jessop declared that the examination of the state's production, or, as he phrased it, the "historical variability of statehood," was one of the defining themes of current research on the state (Jessop 2001). Indeed, there have been a sizable number of publications that have put the production of the state into question.

In terms of intellectual trajectories, the vast majority of these works have followed from the concerns of postcolonial theory and/or insights derived from structuralist and poststructuralist thought. Two of the earliest and most notable examples of this trend, Dario Melossi (1990) and Timothy Mitchell (1991), follow along Foucauldian lines. More recently from within that general trajectory are works from Stefano Harney (2002) and Mark Neocleous (2003). Within the confines of anthropology, Michael Taussig's (1997) and Michael Herzfeld's (1992) studies are seminal examples of an increasingly growing trend toward ethnographic work on the production of the state.[5] Along more historiographic lines there have been a number of significant studies examining the production of the state, perhaps the most rigorous and direct being Fernando Coronil's work on Venezuela (1997) (see also Joseph and Nugent 1994). In addition there are a great many studies within the domains of comparative literature and cultural studies that seek to uncover parts of the processes that produce the state, especially in relation to the issues of identity and the national community.[6] Among the few contributions that remain outside the domain of the post-

---

[5] See Das and Poole (2004) and Hansen and Stepputat (2001) for examples of recent works along these lines.

[6] Notable examples include such paradigmatic works as Benedict Anderson's *Imagined Communities* (1991), Homi Bhabha's influential collection (1990), and Stathis Gourgouris's impressive study of the creation of modern Greece (1996).

colonial and poststructuralist theory are those by Joel Migdal (2001) and Pierre Bourdieu (1996).

In a parallel tendency, there have been many recent works that attempt to uncover the state's ontological status within the context of globalization. Michael Hardt and Antonio Negri (2000) have famously argued that the nation-state is being superseded by the logic of empire. Many others have argued that the nation-state becomes less relevant as global political arrangements subvert its autonomy and lead to broader, transnational forms of governance.[7] Much about the state is being discussed and examined within the globalization literature, but what is most significant in this context is how the existence of the state has been put into question, how our experiences of globalization are leading us to question its actuality and future.

Thus we have two groups of literature, each emerging in the early 1990s, that, in stark contrast to previous trends, are skeptical toward the state, that see it as something that is temporary and contingent. It is no coincidence that leftist youth today are drawn toward anarchism much more strongly than to Marxism or other competing traditions. This newfound skepticism toward the state that our experiences of globalization have helped instill in us is rapidly reshaping the contours of political inquiry.[8] As such, these trends in political inquiry have not been some scholastic whim but are deeply connected to the vicissitudes of the current political situation, not unlike the previous surges in research on the state. Although this work may differ from the theoretical positions of many of the aforementioned studies of the state, it has emerged from similar practical concerns and out of this same newfound skepticism.

What differentiates the present study from more ethnographic studies and those that come out of area studies is that it is attempting to address similar questions but in a completely inverse style. Leaving aside the globalization literature, almost all the works in the new literature on the production of the state, grounded as they are in ethnography and the case study method, attempt to address the general from the point of view of the particular. The method adopted here is exactly the opposite, to come up with some kind of general theory, or at least an outline of a theory, before attempting to explain the many particular cases that may exist.[9] This style of inquiry, which follows from the general principle that social analysis should proceed from the abstract toward the concrete,

---

[7] Significant examples include Shaw (2000) and Strange (1996).

[8] Postcolonial theory is privileged in this context in that, from the point of view of the colonized, the state has often been experienced as a contingent product of a political project and not as some essential and natural thing. It is not surprising that postcolonial theory has been at the forefront of questioning the state and examining its production. However, on the level of concept formation, postcolonial theory has not lived up to its possibilities.

[9] This point is in the tradition of concept formation characteristic of such thinkers as Marx, Weber, and Wilhelm Dilthey as well as more contemporary theorists such as Canguilhem and Foucault.

has tended to fall by the wayside in the current fashions of postmodernism, where "grand theories" are derided and the idea of "totality" has been abandoned. The present study takes the viewpoint that we can indeed still speak of social totalities and only when placed into this context do we fully come to grips with the social significance of the great assortment of "particular" facts and events that the current engagements with the question of the state's production have uncovered.

> The interconnectedness and mediatedness of the parts and the whole also signifies that isolated facts are abstractions, artificially uprooted moments of a whole which become concrete and true only when set in the respective whole. Similarly, a whole whose moments have not been differentiated and determined is merely an abstract, empty whole. (Kosík 1976, 22)

As such, the focus here is not to explain any particular existing state or even any particular "type" of state (industrial, postcolonial, Keynesian, fascist, etc.). It is to come to grips with the general contours of the question, to understand its presuppositions, subquestions, and challenges.

The task of explaining the state is not one that can be adequately and decisively accomplished by one person or in the scope of a single monograph. It is an ongoing project that necessarily involves much research and continued theoretical exploration and refinement. Here the immediate goal is to come up with some idea of the whole and the parts when it comes to the state, to develop a sufficiently materialist conception and description of the state so that we can finally move forward with the task of explanation. In many ways, the present work is more like an outline toward a theory of the state, a schematic overview of the questions and categories that a properly materialist theory of the state can be founded upon.

1

The Spontaneous Theory of the State and the State as Spontaneous Theory

Sometimes we stand in wonder before a chosen object; we build up hypotheses and reveries; in this way we form convictions which have all the appearance of true knowledge. . . . In point of fact, scientific objectivity is possible only if one has broken first with the immediate object, if one has refused to yield to the seduction of the initial choice, if one has checked and contradicted the thoughts which arise from one's first observation. . . . Far from marveling at the object, objective thought must treat it ironically.

—Gaston Bachelard, *The Psychoanalysis of Fire*

That Marxist state theory should be silent on the question of the state's production is shocking for two reasons. Firstly, Marxist theory has always held the position that its goal is not simply to make sense of the world, but to change it, to transform reality through a critical and demystifying understanding of it.[1] A "philosophy of praxis" (Gramsci) or "class struggle in theory" (Althusser) is the intended character of such a theoretical project; Marxist political theory takes as its goal the transformation of society through the production of a critical and subversive understanding of it.[2] Indeed, irrespective of the degree of success, the production of critical knowledge has been an explicit goal for state theory.[3]

---

[1] Etienne Balibar notes this point in his discussion of Marx's analysis of the commodity form: "What, then, is Marx's objective in describing the phenomenon in this way? It is twofold. On the one hand, by a movement akin to demystification or demythification, he is concerned to *dissolve* that phenomenon, to show that it is an appearance based, in the last instance, on a 'misunderstanding.' The phenomena just mentioned (exchange-value considered as a property of objects, the autonomous movement of commodities and prices) will have to be traced back to a *real* cause which has been masked and the effect of which has been inverted" (as in a *camera obscura*) (Balibar 1995, 60).

[2] Slavoj Žižek has summarized this particular component of Marxist thought: "In short, in Marxism as well as in psychoanalysis we encounter what Althusser calls *topique*, the topical character of thought. This topicality does not concern only or even primarily the fact that the object of thought has to be conceived as a complex Whole of instances that

Second, it was Marx himself who first noted the tendency for political theory to misrecognize the state as being universal and ahistorical. In his "Contribution to the Critique of Hegel's *Philosophy of Right*" Marx argued that Hegel's misrecognition of the state as universal and as possessing a privileged ontological status in relation to "civil society" functioned to legitimize the state. As Jean Hyppolite has noted:

> When, in turn, Marx criticizes Hegel for having opposed bourgeois or civil society to the State, for having arrived by deduction at the constitutional monarchy and Prussian democracy, giving them an aspect of the eternal, he is simply revealing an essential tendency of Hegelian thought, which is to legitimate existing reality by conceiving it philosophically. ... The truly concrete subject, the bearer of predicates, is *man as social being*, who belongs to what Hegel called bourgeois society, and the State, which Hegel mistakenly took for the Subject, as Idea, is in fact a predicate of man's social nature. The Idea—in reality, the product of man's social activity—appears in Hegel as the authentic which results in "a mystery which degenerates into mystification," as Marx puts it. (Hyppolite 1969, 108–112)

This straightforward and powerful opposition to the Hegelian view of the state has tended to be forgotten by a Marxist state theory that has largely been content

---

cannot be reduced to some identical underlying Ground (the intricate interplay of base in superstructure in Marxism; of Ego, Superego and Id in psychoanalysis). "Topicality," rather, refers to *the topical character of 'thought' itself*: theory is always part of the conjunction into which it intervenes. The 'object' of Marxism is society, yet 'class struggle in theory' means that the ultimate theme of Marxism is the 'material force of ideas'—that is, the way Marxism itself *qua* revolutionary theory transforms its object (brings about the emergence of the revolutionary subject, etc.). . . . In short, a 'topic' theory fully acknowledges the short circuit between the theoretical frame and an element within this frame: theory itself is a moment of the totality that is its 'object'" (Žižek 1994, 182).
[3] For example, Ralph Miliband framed *The State in Capitalist Society* as a critical response to the pluralist hegemony inside and outside the academy (cf. Miliband 1969, 1–7). Nicos Poulantzas intended *Political Power and Social Classes* to be for the political moment of the capitalist mode of production what Marx's *Capital* was for its economic moment: a rigorous and demystifying understanding of its specificity and dynamics (cf. Poulantzas 1973, 16–23; Jessop 1985, 59–60). Even behind the presumed obscurity and theoreticism of their debate, we see that Poulantzas stressed the critical function rather than simply the methodological or epistemological content of Miliband's arguments. The essence of Poulantzas's critique of Miliband is that he fails to sufficiently demystify the state.

to debate the class functions of the state while ignoring key questions regarding its ontological status and historical specificities.[4]

Of course, no Marxist state theorist says that the state is an a priori, that its existence is not a product of social relations or practices, that it does not have a cause. Nonetheless, state theory acts "as if" this were the case. Precisely because state theory does not explain the existence of the state, because state theory takes the state as its point of departure and fails to demystify its existence through explanation, all state theory proceeds "as if" the state was indeed a universal a priori predicate to our social existence rather than a product of our social existence. This "as if" act by state theory is a fetishizing act (and thus reifies the state) because it endows the state with ontological qualities not its own and abstracts its existence from the realm of social relations.[5]

The State as Subject and as Object

This reification is present in both dominant conceptualizations of the state within Marxist and neo-Weberian state theory: the state as subject and the state as object. State-as-subject conceptualizations understand the state to be a social actor distinguished by a common subjectivity among the people who occupy state positions. In its Leninist form, this conceptualization considers the state to be an appendage of the bourgeoisie by virtue of the bourgeois class consciousness of those who "control" the state (cf. Lenin 1932). For Lenin, the state functions as an "instrument" of class domination.[6] For the state to be an instrument of class domination, however, a certain class consciousness must be presupposed on the part of those who control state power. The "instrument" is not the state in this context but, rather, state power. This is to say, in all theories that conceive of state power as a thing (instrumentalist theories of power), the state institutions must be unified by a given subjectivity for state power itself to gain coherence and unity.

---

[4] Paul Thomas has suggested that a return Marx's early work, particularly his critique of Hegel, would be of great benefit to state theory precisely because of the ways that Marx opposes Hegel's view of the state as a "finished thing" (cf. Thomas 1994, 27–49). In a similar way, Stathis Kouvelakis returns to the Marx of the early 1840s in order to discover his theory of the state and politics, coming to conclusions very similar to Thomas's regarding the significance of Marx's break with Hegel vis-à-vis the theory of the state (cf. Kouvelakis 2003, 246–256).

[5] See Lukacs (1971, esp. 83–110) and Žižek (1989, ch. 1) for an extended discussion of reification and fetishization.

[6] This understanding of the Leninist theory of the state goes against most categorizations of it. Most commentators focus on the claim that the state is an instrument of class domination and categorize Lenin's conception of the state as being "instrumentalist," that Lenin considers the state to be an instrument/thing/object (cf. Jessop 1990, 28). There is no doubt that Lenin is an instrumentalist, but, as I argue below, instrumentalist theories of power result in a state-as-subject conception of the state since only in this way can the unity of state institutions and the coherent function of state power be understood.

The most cogent example of this Leninist concept of the state as subject can be found in Miliband's *The State in Capitalist Society*. Miliband concurrently emphasizes the institutional fragmentation of state power and the importance of the "state elite" in giving direction and coherence to this potentially fragmented power:

> There is one preliminary problem about the state which is very seldom considered, yet which requires attention if the discussion of its nature and role is to be properly focused. This is the fact that "the state" is not a thing, that it does not, as such, exist. What "the state" stands for is a number of particular institutions which, together, constitute its reality, and which interact as part of what may be called the state system. (Miliband 1969, 49)

> These are the institutions—the government, the administration, the military and the police, the judicial branch, subcentral government and parliamentary assemblies—which make up "the state," and whose interrelationship shapes the form of the state system. It is these institutions in which "state power" lies, and it is through them that this power is wielded in its different manifestations by the people who occupy the leading positions in each of these institutions. (Miliband 1969, 54)

Having established the fragmented nature of the state and state power, emphasis must be placed upon the agency of this state elite in uniting these institutions and for "wielding" state power in a coherent way. The consciousness of this state elite is what must be examined for Miliband if we are to be able to characterize the state as a coherent actor. To these ends, he examines the class origins, social networks, and educational attributes that characterize all state elites. It is upon that basis that he is able to conclude that the state is a bourgeois actor.

> The reason for attaching considerable importance to the social composition of the state elite in advanced capitalist countries lies in the strong presumption which this creates as to its general outlook, ideological disposition and political bias. (Miliband 1969, 68)

> What the evidence conclusively suggests is that in terms of social origin, education and class situation, the men who have manned *all* command positions in the state system have largely, and in many cases overwhelmingly, been drawn from the world of business and property, or from the professional middle classes. (Miliband 1969, 66)

Thus, a central concept for Miliband is what he calls "bourgeoisification," which he uses to argue that even those members of the state elite who do not come from the bourgeois class itself undergo a process of education and socialization through which they learn to think like those who are members of the bourgeoisie.

In its neo-Weberian form, the state-as-subject conceptualization considers the state to be a distinct actor by virtue of the bureaucratic rationality that unites its members and that provides a socially autonomous set of interests such members act to maximize (cf. Block 1987; Skocpol 1979 and 1985; and Levi 1988). Unlike its Leninist counterpart, such theories posit the autonomy of the state from society, since the subjectivity that unites its members is state specific and does not originate within society, state managers have a subjectivity that is all their own.

Notable contemporary versions of such arguments can be found in the work of Theda Skocpol and Fred Block. Block rejects more orthodox Marxist theories of the state since they assume a class consciousness among the bourgeoisie that he claims is reductionist and remains unexplained (Block 1987, 52–58). As a corrective, Block puts forth an argument that does not rely on such assumptions and that, he claims, does a better job of explaining what objective processes determine why the state does what it does. In doing this, Block privileges three groups, capitalists, workers, and the managers of the state, as being the principal agents behind state policy. Capitalists and workers are assumed not to have a class consciousness; they are guided by their individual economic interests. State managers are assumed to share a set of interests (namely, the preservation and expansion of the state) given their position within the institutions of the state and are expected to act in ways that further these interests. This is to say that it is assumed that the individual interests of state managers can be reduced to their institutional interests (bureaucratic rationality). Similarly, Skocpol argues that the state is best understood as having interests of its own that make its rationality autonomous from the rationality of social actors (Skocpol 1979, 24–33).

The fetish in the above neo-Weberian approaches is an institutionalist one. State managers, it is argued, share a bureaucratic rationality, which explains the given subjectivity of this state as actor. This rationality (or, subjectivity) is a function of the institutional position of these individuals. If you or I occupied one of these positions, it would be expected that we too would then "think" and "act" in accordance with this bureaucratic rationality. Thus, we could say, the state as an autonomous social agent exists when those individuals who occupy the positions of state managers share a bureaucratic rationality and act accordingly. However, this relation between the position of an individual within the institutions of the state and their "bureaucratic" consciousness remains unexplained. It is assumed that the state exists since it is assumed that any person who occupies an institutional position within the state acquires this bureaucratic rationality. At no point does Block or Skocpol explain how this actually happens and what conditions are necessary for this process to be successful.[7] Institutions become substituted for state managers. Such neo-Weberian theories talk about institutions acting "as if" these institutions were thinking, calculating agents even though the Weberian assumptions they share place the methodological emphasis on state managers qua individuals and not on institutions as such.[8] In this way, neo-Weberian theories of the state as subject are guilty of presupposing and reifying the state.

Leninist theories are also guilty of this presupposition and reification since they presume that these individuals share a class consciousness without explaining how this may happen and what conditions are necessary for this process to be successful. A direct correspondence between class origins and consciousness is assumed but never explained or understood.[9] The state as subject is presumed by such theorists and the state gains the appearance of an entity that exists beyond the society itself since its existence is not grounded upon any particular set of social practices or conditions.

State-as-object definitions reduce the state to a set of institutions that constitute the site of political struggle and antagonism between various social actors. The state does not act but is, rather, a material site acted upon. Such definitions are common to structuralist theories of the state (or, theories that share a relational theory of power). The early work of Nicos Poulantzas and that of Louis Althusser are prime examples of this concept.

In such formulations, the state and its functions are determined by the reproductive requisites of the given social whole. The state exists as a region of any given social formation and functions according to the needs of the social formation to reproduce its constitutive relations (cf. Althusser 1969, ch.3). In

---

[7] Skocpol makes some attempt to overcome this in her latter work when she stresses the necessity that state officials share "a unified sense of ideological purpose" for the state to be an autonomous actor (Skocpol 1985). This, however, remains "outside" of her theory since she is unable to examine how this happens. It remains an unexplained external variable that, at best, qualifies claims to state autonomy by positing certain conditions that are necessary but not sufficient for such autonomy to exist.

[8] "For sociological purposes, however, the phenomenon 'the state' does not consist necessarily or even primarily of the elements which are relevant to legal analysis; and for sociological purposes there is no such thing as a collective personality which 'acts.' When reference is made in a sociological context to a state, a nation, a corporation, a family, or an army corps, or to similar collectives, what is meant is, on the contrary, *only* a certain kind of development of actual or possible social actions of persons" (Weber 1978, 14).

[9] Pierre Bourdieu's *The State Nobility* (1996) is promising in this respect in that, although not sharing the problematic common to this Leninist conception of the state, it examines the various institutions and practices (at least in France) through which individuals come to be constituted as part of the ruling class that manages the state. This work in many ways overlaps Miliband's emphasis on "bourgeoisification" but addresses the question in a much more detailed way and avoids the fetishizing assumptions noted above.

Althusser's formulation, this is accomplished by the combination of the ideological and repressive state apparatuses, which function to secure and reproduce the necessary ideological dispositions and coerce the dominated classes (Althusser 1971). In Poulantzas's version, this is accomplished through a relatively autonomous state that functions to unify capitalists into a coherent class and to separate the working class into individuals (Poulantzas 1973). In both cases this is a product of class power being mediated through state institutions and forms.

These theories also reify the state since they take it to be a logical necessity that functions according to some omnipotent knowledge of the reproductive needs of capitalism. The state exists as one of the assumed three regions of all social formations (the economic, the cultural/ideological, and the political) whose functions are overdetermined by its relations to the social whole (structural causality). As such, these theories not only fail to question the historical, and thus contingent, material conditions that the existence of the state is grounded upon but, in formalist fashion, present arbitrary and purely analytical distinctions (political, cultural, economic) as corresponding to real and ontologically privileged spheres of society that are relatively autonomous.[10]

A Note on Philip Abrams and Ontology

This tendency for state theory to reify the state had been noted by Philip Abrams (1988) in an article that was originally written in 1977. He argued that political sociology, particularly Marxist state theory, has reified the state by presenting it as something that exists in the strong sense of the term. For Abrams, the true mode of existence of the state is not material but ideological; the state does not exist. What exists is the belief that the state exists. The obvious reason for this misrecognition, Abrams argues, is its legitimating function of concealing the true, class, basis, and functions of political power.

> The state is, then, in every sense of the term a triumph of concealment. It conceals the real history and relations of subjection behind an ahistorical mask of legitimating illusion; contrives to deny the existence of connections and conflicts which would if recognized be incompatible with the claimed autonomy and integration of the state. (Abrams 1988, 77)

Abrams's critique is at once a great advancement and regression. His critique was the first to take contemporary political inquiry to task for its failure to question the existence of the state. Moreover, his assertion that the belief in

---

[10] Gramsci noted the danger of confusing methodological categories with organic ones in his comments on economism: "The approach of the free trade movement is based on a theoretical error whose practical origin is not hard to identify: namely the distinction between political society and civil society, which is made and presented as an organic one, whereas in fact it is merely methodological" (Gramsci 1971, 160).

the existence of the state is a fundamental and neglected issue is an important political and theoretical challenge. Nonetheless, the methodological tone and implications of his argument are in many ways a regression within social inquiry. By asserting that the state does not exist, by assuming that the belief in the state's existence is simply an illusion, Abrams fails to recognize the state as a social fact, as something with social existence. The important question in regard to the state's existence is not a yes or no ontological one; as Antonio Negri puts it, "Existence is not a problem. The immediacy of being reveals itself in nonproblematic terms to the pure intellect" (Negri 1991, 45). The important question, as already indirectly indicated, is not whether or not the state exists per se but whether it exists as a social or a natural fact. The critical task of state theory is to explain and demystify the processes and practices that produce the social existence of the state and thus to negate the state's claim to universality and naturalness.

On this issue Abrams would have greatly benefited from going back to Marx and Weber or forward to Deleuze and Guattari. Rather than separate the material existence of a given object from the "belief in its existence" or the abstract categories that refer to it, as Abrams does, all of the foregoing theorists emphasize the function of such categories toward the social existence of an object. Marx's analysis of economic categories illustrates this point quite well (Marx 1970, 205–214). Marx asserted that conceptual categories are not simply neutral references to some already (non)existing object but are an integral part of the object itself (cf. Ollman 1971, ch. 2).

> Just as in general when examining any historical or social science, so also in the case of the development of economic categories is it always necessary to remember that the subject, in this context contemporary bourgeois society, is presupposed both in reality and in the mind, and that therefore categories express forms of existence and conditions of existence—and sometimes merely separate aspects of this particular society, the subject. (Marx 1970, 212)

Weber's famous definition of the state also reveals this point if we read it carefully.[11] What is particular to the state is not violence, or its territorialization, but the legitimacy of such violence and dominating command-obey relationships: "If the state is to exist, the dominated must obey the authority claimed by the powers that be" (Weber 1958, 78). If force must be legitimate in order for the state to exist, then the cognitive and affectual processes that create this legitimacy must be of primary interest. On this issue Weber, as had Marx, stresses the

---

[11] "A state is a human community that (successfully) claims the *monopoly of the legitimate use of physical force* within a given territory" (Weber 1958, 78).

necessity to understand the objectifying function of categories in the production of what we take to be reality:

> It is necessary for us to forego here a detailed discussion of the case which is by far the most complicated and most interesting, namely, the problem of the logical structure of the *concept of the state*. The following however should be noted: when we inquire as to what corresponds to the idea of the "state" in empirical reality, we find an infinity of diffuse and discrete human actions, both active and passive, factually and legally regulated relationships, partly unique and partly recurrent in character, all bound together by an idea, namely, the belief in the actual or normative validity of rules and of the authority-relationships of some human beings towards others. (Weber 1949, 99)

> So-called "objectivity"—and Weber never speaks of objectivity except as "so-called" and in quotation marks—"rests exclusively on the fact that the given reality is ordered in categories, which are *subjective* in the specific sense that they constitute the *precondition* of our knowledge and are contingent upon the presupposition of the value of that particular truth which only empirical knowledge can give us." (Lowith 1993, 53–54)

From this, we could deduce that the existence of the state is contingent upon the meaning-creating function of such objectifying categories and that these objectifying processes are what must be understood if we are to understand the material basis of the state. Indeed, Deleuze and Guattari, from a radically different epistemological position, have come to exactly the same conclusion.

> There is thus an image of thought covering all of thought; it is the special object of "noology" and is like the State-form developed in thought. . . . It is easy to see what thought gains from this: a gravity it would never have on its own, a center that makes everything, including the State, appear to exist by its own efficacy or on its own sanction. But the State gains just as much. Indeed, by developing in thought in this way the State-form gains something essential: a whole consensus. Only thought is capable of inventing the fiction of a State that is universal by right, of elevating the State to de jure universality. (Deleuze and Guattari 1987, 374–375)

Of course, these qualifications do not take us very far from Abrams's argument on the importance of explaining the state-idea and of noting its delu-

sional effects. The whole set of these concerns becomes recast, however, because the state-idea is no longer a mask, an "irrational" belief or a false consciousness on the part of those (other than the bourgeoisie, for whom this belief
is of great benefit) who believe in it. The state-idea is concurrent with the real
qua social existence of the state. For example, a great deal of Abrams's claim
that the state does not exist derives from his assertion that there is no unity of
"state" institutions that would constitute them as a state:

> We may reasonably infer that the state as a special object of
> social analysis does not exist as a real entity. . . . Political in-
> stitutions, especially in the enlarged sense of Miliband's state-
> system, conspicuously fail to display a unity of practice—just
> as they constantly discover their inability to function as a more
> general factor of cohesion. Manifestly they are divided against
> one another, volatile and confused. (Abrams 1988, 79)[12]

The assertion that there is no unity of practice between state institutions, by no
means a "reasonable inference," implies that such a unity could only be the outcome of something inside each institution, some kind of state essence or unity of
purpose, that unites them in a substantive way. At the least, Abrams assumes, in
surprisingly unhistorical fashion, that state institutions inherently cannot function in a coherent way. This conclusion, however, conflicts with the assumed
dominance of the state-idea. The conclusion that there is or is not a unity of
practice is contingent on our subjective determination of what constitutes a unity
of practice. The state-idea may create a unity of practice and solidify the role of
the state as a factor of cohesion by creating points of view and cognitive categories among citizens and state managers that do function as factors of cohesion
and do result in there being a unity of practice. If we believe in the state-idea,
the state has achieved its function as a factor of cohesion, and its practices will
be judged to be united given the appropriate categorization of them. Even things
as apparently unrelated as wine and sociology may be united by placing both
under the category "French." Just by being "state" institutions, political institutions gain unity and cohesion.

A related shortcoming is Abrams's lack of explanation regarding the
propensity of people to believe in the state-idea. We are left with the image of
members of the dominated classes foolishly believing in a fiction put forth by
bourgeois propagandists. That even Marxist theorists should have engaged in
this reification and misrecognition is in need of explanation and is obviously a
crucial part of any attempt to explain the state-idea. When Abrams does attempt
to explain the propensity of theorists to reify the state he makes the argument

---

[12] Gianfranco Poggi has made a similar argument regarding the lack of cohesion among
state apparatuses (1990, 184).

that the belief in the state-idea results from some methodological mania and strategic irrationality.

> It is worth considering why Marxism generally should have proved so susceptible to this sort of ambiguity. I think it results from an unresolved tension between Marxist theory and Marxist practice. Marxist theory needs the state as an abstract-formal object in order to explain the integration of class societies. . . . all [Marxist theorists] are hypnotised by the brilliant effect of standing Hegel the right way up, of discovering the state as the political concentration of class relationships. . . . At the same time Marxist practice needs the state as a real-concrete object, the immediate object of political struggle. Marxist political practice is above all a generation of political class struggle over and above economic struggle. . . . In effect to opt for political struggle thus becomes a matter of participating in the ideological construction of the state as a real entity. (Abrams 1988, 70)

As with the assertion that the state-idea is a mask foolishly believed in by the masses, to imply that Marxist theorists tend toward irrationality, that they are "hypnotized," fails to identify any rational causes that may explain these tendencies. A more appropriate explanation for the belief in the state-idea is attempted further below.

It is important to note that some of the problems identified so far have been at least partly addressed by Nicos Poulantzas in his later work and, subsequently, by Bob Jessop. It is with Jessop and Poulantzas that state theory begins to explain the existence of the state by looking to practices and strategies that may serve as its causes. This not only represents the beginning of a theory that does not fetishize the state but also addresses related shortcomings regarding the unity/disunity of institutions. With Abrams as with state-as-subject theorists (Miliband, Block, Skocpol, etc.) the unity/disunity of the state was assumed. As can be noted from the discussion below, Poulantzas and Jessop understand the substantive unity of state institutions to be historically contingent and thus an empirical question that cannot be assumed away. This advancement coincides with Poulantzas's movement away from the more formalistic elements of structuralism and his subsequent definition of the state as a social relation.

The State as a Social Relation

There is no question that Poulantzas's most famous concept, "the relative autonomy of the capitalist state," tends to be among the least understood. In part, this confusion stems from comparing the concept of relative autonomy to neo-Weberian claims that the state has complete autonomy from society, the resulting assumption being that relative autonomy must imply a limited version of that argument, some but not complete autonomy from society. Poulantzas never implied any autonomy of the state from society (Poulantzas even rejects the state-society dichotomy). Relative autonomy always referred to autonomy from particular class interests, not society as a whole. For this reason, political power is always class power; there is no "state" power in the sense of a power separate or autonomous from social classes.[13] The conceptual problem was to understand how the state can act against some narrow or short-term interests of capitalists in order to act in their general or class interests. In *Political Power and Social Classes*, Poulantzas explains relative autonomy as an outcome of structural causality; the multiple relations of the political to the social whole overdetermine its functions, and it will have a relative autonomy vis-à-vis the economic and cultural moments of the social whole since they all affect each other and, thus, will also have a relative autonomy from particular class interests since only in this way can the social whole be reproduced. This explanation was quickly abandoned, however, and Poulantzas's definition of the state as object (or, region, as he would term it) was replaced with the definition of the state as a social relation.

Poulantzas defined the state in *State, Power, Socialism* as a social relation:

> *A relationship of forces, or more precisely the material condensation of such a relationship among classes and class fractions, such as this is expressed within the State in a necessarily specific form* . . . by grasping the State as the condensation of a *relationship*, we avoid the impasse of that eternal counterposition of the State as a Thing-instrument and the State as a Subject. (Poulantzas 1978, 129)

This definition should be combined with Poulantzas's class ontology where classes are to be found only as class struggles and practices: "social classes do not firstly exist as such, and only then enter into a class struggle. Social classes coincide with class practices" (Poulantzas 1975, 14). This represents Poulantzas's attempt to move away from class in-itself and for-itself definitions since social class is neither a product of academic definition nor a result of the subjective dispositions of "class" actors. Poulantzas's definition of state and class leads to the conclusion that what he terms the "institutional materiality" of the state is a historical product of a multiplicity of class practices and struggles. This allows us to pose the question of what material causes and processes underpin the exis-

---

[13] Even David Held tends towards this confusion of Poulantzas when he agues that to claim relative autonomy and to posit that all power is class power is contradictory: "There are, however, inconsistencies in Poulantzas's formulation . . . where he at one and the same time grants a certain autonomy to the state and argues that all power is class power" (Held 1989, 70).

tence of the state. Thus, in contrast to previous theories of the state, Poulantzas presents a view of the state that does not reify it.

The explanation of relative autonomy and of the unity of the state institutions is revised in light of this definition of the state as a social relation. Relative autonomy becomes a product of the class struggles since, within and between state institutions, various classes and class factions are engaged in struggle and, thus, no one class will have complete control of all the state institutions. The product of past struggles will be materialized in the state institutions themselves, their structures, rules, procedures, etc. The class bias these institutions exhibit because of these previous political struggles is what Poulantzas terms, following Claus Offe (cf. Offe 1973), structural selectivity; the selectivity the institutions display toward and against various possible laws and policies.

The historically contingent balance of forces between the classes represented within the state institutions (what Poulantzas terms the "power bloc") will dictate the particular degree and content of this relative autonomy. If a unity of the state institutions exists, it is to be found in the hegemonic position of one institution (and the class fraction that dominates it) over the other institutions. The hegemonic institution and class interests it represents is able to coordinate the actions of the other state institutions through its power over them as well as the corresponding agreements and concessions reached by the members of the power bloc. In short, the cause of the unity of the state and its relative autonomy is class struggle.

In *State Theory* (1990), Jessop offers the most recent and elaborate discussion within the trajectory opened by Poulantzas. He asserts that the state as a social relation can be analyzed as the site, generator, and product of strategies. First, understanding the state as the site of strategy implies substituting the Offean notion of "structural selectivity" for the concept of "strategic selectivity." Jessop argues that the concept of structural selectivity ignores the differential impact of the state on the capacity of class-relevant forces to pursue their interests; although the state may be more open to some policies and less to others, it does not display this selectivity irrespective of the ways class forces pursue their policy preferences. The concept of "strategic selectivity" brings out more clearly the relational aspect of this selectivity as a product of the relationship between state forms and the strategies that different forces adopt toward the state. In other words, strategic selectivity radicalizes the contingency of the ways by which the form of the state participates in the production of class domination; it is not only the form of the state that plays that role, but also the various strategies and their potential and actual success that condition this selectivity and allow us to identify it. In summary, states are not neutral sites with reference to political strategies of social forces, but are more open to some political strategies than others (Jessop 1990, 9–12). Second, the state is also a generator of political strategies. In order for the state to be interpreted as possessing substantive unity, it is not sufficient, Jessop argues, to establish its formal unity—this is the case with subjectivist theories. The unity of the state, the nature of its subjectivity, and its capacity to act are to be understood in the light of a reinterpretation of the role of state institutions as producers of political strategies. Third and last, the state's structure is not a set of functional imperatives determined by the societal whole, but it is the product of past political strategies and struggles:

> The current *strategic selectivity* of the state is in part the emergent effect of the interaction between its past patterns of *strategic selectivity* and the strategies adopted for its transformation. (Jessop 1990, 261)

Neither Poulantzas nor Jessop, however, fully overcome the epistemological limits of previous state theories. Although the concept of the state in Poulantzas is made radically contingent, class, class interests, and class power are assumed to exist as its necessary precondition. That is, Poulantzas never justifies why the practices that produce the state are necessarily and exclusively class practices. Furthermore, it is not very clear what types of practices and mechanisms translate the materiality of classes and class power into the institutional materiality of the state. Yet, by transforming the state into the point of arrival of state theory, Poulantzas's relational theory denies the state any a priori existence. The state exists, for Poulantzas, but its existence is a contingency of specific articulations of power relations.

In Jessop's strategic theory of the state, the inconclusive status of Poulantzas's concept of "social relation" is given clearer contours. He attempts to overcome Poulantzas's class reductionism by assigning materiality solely to institutions. Although these concepts are produced within an immanently contingency-oriented framework—thus denying the predetermined nature of functional imperatives and subjectivity—Jessop's threefold characterization of the state still reduces that concept to the institutional materiality of society. The state, therefore, can only exist when there is substantive unity among state institutions. But how are we to know what "state" institutions are? We could choose a point in time where the state-as-institutional order exists and identify its component institutions that we could then label as "state" institutions. But, then again, how could we know if the state-as-institutional order exists if we do not know what institutions to look to in order to establish the existence and form of their unity? Obviously, at some point we must posit what "state" institutions are a priori. Ultimately, substituting the materiality qua objectivity of institutions for the materiality qua objectivity of classes does not fully overcome the problems related to Poulantzas's reductionism nor does it fully overcome the epistemological limits of state theory since it still assumes the existence of "state" institutions if not the state itself.

From the Reification of the State to Its Explanation

That the state has been reified by Marxist and neo-Weberian theorists cannot be a matter of chance or lack of thought. It must be symptomatic of a particular quality that the state possesses that makes it difficult to treat "ironically"; it must be symptomatic of the hold the state has over our theoretical and political imagination. The state is for political theorists what fire was for the alchemists of the premodern era. In both cases, the seductive power of the object over the imagination of those who attempt to explain it results in metaphorical and incomplete theories (cf. Bachelard 1987, 59–82). In both cases, myths and folklore are the privileged form of our understanding. From Prometheus and fire-bellied birds we have gone to tales of social contracts, George Washington, and the Battle of Kosovo.

If, as Bachelard argues, the experience of fire's heat, light, smoke, etc. limits one's ability to explain it scientifically, then we could also assume that the source of our inability to explain the state in sufficiently objective ways (or, at least, in ways that do not reify it) is our experience of the state. We know from Marx, Weber, Mauss, and, especially, Durkheim that while in our social existence we develop commonsense understandings of various phenomena, the first goal of a social science is to break with these preconceived notions and reconstruct them as "social facts."[14] Perhaps a telling indicator of the difficulty of accomplishing this break in relation to the state is the difficulty of identifying "state" experiences. What is our experience of the "state"? Is it the delivery of mail? The presence of traffic regulations? The collection of taxes? The presence of national borders?

Weber's claim, as quoted earlier, that "when we inquire as to what corresponds to the idea of the 'state' in empirical reality, we find an infinity of diffuse and discrete human actions . . . all bound together by an idea" is not only startling from the perspective of what his concept of the state is usually thought to be, but it is also suggestive of the sublime quality proper to the state. If Weber is right, it is through the eye and mind of the citizen that the state comes into existence. Moreover, those characteristics of "human actions" that qualify them as inclusive of the state are not inherent to the actions themselves but rather to the motivations and perceptions of these actions. The assertion that actions may contain within them something beyond their physical characteristics and that this something is to be found within the realm of ideas suggests, in more Marxist terms, that the state exists primarily as a fetish. Here, the state emerges as a very different kind of object than that which we are used to. Fire, irrespective of cultural differences, education, ideologies, and so forth, is experienced in the usual sense, as an object that, by way of our sensory perceptions, results in a feeling, a change in the physical state of the body: warmth, fear, pain, and so on. This is to say, the problem with fire is presymbolic; it is not a question of the way ideology, or the symbolic order, maps the terrain of experience. It is not a quality of this or that culture that leads us to misrecognize fire, but rather it is a product of the material characteristics of fire itself that lead us to develop cultural artifacts and ways of thinking that make it difficult to develop scientific explanations.

---

[14] See Bourdieu, Chamboredon, and Passeron (1991, esp. 13–55) for an extended discussion of this issue.

The state can never be experienced in such a way, since the very categorization of phenomenon as "state" phenomenon is necessarily prior to its return in the form of a palpable confirmation (experience) of that initial categorization. There is no "state" experience prior to the existence and use of the category "state." Here, we arrive at Žižek's definition of a "sublime object." Beyond the physical characteristics of an object, an abstract quality, one secured by the symbolic order, can come to be ascribed to it—raising the functional status of that object to an acute level of ideological importance (cf. Žižek 1989).[15]

The ideological and cognitive importance of the "state" in contemporary life is paramount. As Poulantzas notes, "we cannot imagine any social phenomena (any knowledge, power, language or writing) as posed in a state prior to the State: for all social reality must stand in relation to the State and to class divisions" (Poulantzas 1978, 39).[16] Even the most basic of social scientific concepts, society, seems to be unthinkable without standing it in relation to the state; the state is already assumed as its opposite or its modifier. "Society" either has meaning and specificity in relation to the "state" (state-society or public-private) or in conjunction with a "state" as its modifying pronoun (American society, French society, etc). These two uses of the state category, to map the internal and external limits of what is thought to be society, indicate the importance of explaining the state idea for any attempt to go beyond the spontaneous and ideological understanding that society has of itself.

Of course, the basic reason explaining the ubiquity of this type of categorization is its functionality toward guiding our actions and behaviors. Althusser may be right when he claims that the public-private distinction is only a distinction internal to bourgeois law, that there is no real limit or absence of the state in the name of the "private" or in the name of "civil society" (cf. Althusser 1971, 144). But it is not a product of irrationality that people tend to think in terms of private-public or American society versus French society. These categorizations are of the utmost importance when filing tax returns, planning a trip, organizing a labor union, and so forth.[17] It is precisely for this reason that such concepts have to be rejected. For, although quite useful to our survival in bour-

---

[15] As Žižek notes, the most obvious example of a sublime object in contemporary society is money, with its corresponding fetishizing and cognitive functions (cf. Žižek 1989, 16–21). This point is examined in much more detail in the next chapter.

[16] Cornelius Castoriadis illustrates this point when he argues that our understanding of ancient Greek political thought (especially the concept of the *polis*) is flawed because we are unable to understand without recourse to our modern categories (especially the state) (cf. Castoriadis 1991, ch. 5). This not only shows that "only in relation to the state" can we comprehend social phenomenon but also shows how the state reifies itself in thought, making it appear universal and omnipresent.

[17] As Bourdieu, Chamboredon, and Passeron put it, "These preconceptions or 'prenotions'—'schematic, summary representations' that are 'formed by and for experience'—derive their self-evidence and their 'authority,' as Durkheim observes, from the social functions they fulfill" (Bourdieu, Chamboredon, and Passeron 1991, 13).

geois society, they are prescientific and limit our ability to explain the state since they compel us to constantly presuppose it in order to make sense of the world.

Based on the foregoing, we could go further and say that there is no one "state" idea at all. Rather, the state idea always has two distinct meanings. On the one hand, it refers to the production of the political community in national-territorial terms, mapping the "inside" and "outside" of society. On the other hand, it refers to the formal separation within society of political power from economic power, of "public servant" from "private citizen," of sovereignty from social agency.

What state theory has to do in order to explain the state is to explain the causes of these categorizations, the public-private and the domestic-foreign. Poulantzas's assertion that the state is the product of practices should be taken seriously, and the material causes of the state idea should be sought. The identification of the practices that result in our "state" thinking, and, thus, in the existence of the state and the legitimacy of state power and forms, is the next step for the analytical and strategic progression of Marxist political theory.

The goal of the following chapters is exactly this, to identify and explain how our everyday lives function to produce the state as a social fact. The focus on "everyday life" is intended as a constant reminder that in order to properly explain the state we must look to the social-historical realities and routines of concrete individuals in order to understand how and why the state idea becomes so central and necessary to modern life. In the chapters that follow, the importance and possible causes of each of these two ideological foundations of the state (the division between the public and private, and the formation of the national political community) are addressed. In Chapter 2, I examine how the modern division of the public and private emerges and why it is so necessary to the existence of bourgeois society. The split of the public from private that coincides with the rise of the state in Western Europe is examined as a product of the rise of capitalism and the growth of commodity exchange. The everyday experience of the marketplace as well as the practices the state itself engenders in its regulation of everyday life are presented as the material conditions that explain why the public-private division is so accepted and ubiquitous in modern societies.

Chapter 3 examines the problem of political corruption and how the discourse and legal statutes addressing it both illustrate the fetishized nature of the public sphere and function as symptoms of this public fetish in that the state must constantly police itself and engender practices that "normalize" the presence of the "private" in that which we term the "public." In other words, a close analysis of the problem of political corruption reveals that corruption is a structural attribute of all politics in bourgeois society and that the discourse surrounding political corruption is an attempt to distinguish what is a "normal" presence of private interests in the public sphere and what is a "pathological" presence of the private within the public.

Chapter 4 is a theoretical reworking of the Althusserian concept of interpellation. The conceptual problem of explaining the national political community, it is argued, is a problem of explaining the national individual. How identity is produced from everyday practices is examined, and it is argued that psychoanalysis is a necessary part of any materialist attempt to explain the national individual since it is also necessary to understand the libidinal value of identities in order to explain how some identities are much more politically and ideologically important than others. Chapter 5 is an empirical case study designed to illustrate and further develop the arguments in Chapter 4. The production of the Greek American identity in contemporary New York City is examined.

2

From *The King's Two Bodies* to the Fetish of the Public: The Foundations of the State Abstraction

> The dissociation between the political and the nonpolitical—
> both fictitious and real—is itself political. It is the instrument
> of a policy on which the state power and His Majesty's oppo-
> sition agree. But here the secret is perhaps revealed—it is an
> open secret, the secret of cohesion within incoherence.
> —Henri Lefebvre, *The Explosion*

The *Polis* Versus the State

Before proceeding further, it will be useful to dispose with any remaining uncer-
tainties regarding the state's existence as being universal or particular, natural or
social. The specificity of the state relative to other forms of political organization is an issue that is seldom considered.[1] Explanations of the modern state tend
to be presented as a history of ever-developing state forms moving from the
fractured and not quite rational to increasingly centralized and rationalized
forms (significant examples include Poggi 1978; Tilly 1975; and Giddens
1987).[2] For example, Anthony Giddens (1987), following Eisenstadt (1963) and,
more generally, almost everyone else in contemporary social science, categorizes political forms in terms of the kind of state they represent: national, absolutist, and traditional (all else, from "city-states" and the Aztecs to agrarian empires). These categorizations tend to reflect in practice what was established by
the social contract tradition in principle: the origin of the "state," or "leviathan,"

---

[1] This is not to say that the question is never asked; many theorists from Aristotle to Weber to Negri have placed great importance on the question of political forms. I only mean
to indicate here that the dominant trends in political science and sociology tend to place
emphasis on different forms of the state rather than the state itself as a political form.
[2] There are obvious links between this type of approach and modernization the-
ory/functionalist sociology.

is prehistorical, and it has been a necessary and unavoidable aspect of social life ever since peoples moved out of the primitive chaos of a war-against-all.

Should the term "state" be synonymous with any form of political organization or does it have a specificity that distinguishes itself as a particular and historical phenomenon? The answer to this question will obviously be a product of the analytical goal that underpins a particular approach. If our goal is to emphasize some similarity (i.e., war making and violence) in political forms, an approach such as Giddens's may be appropriate.[3] However, if we want to interrogate the concept of the state in order to uncover the meanings and assumptions it presupposes, the opposite is true since we will want to show that there are particular causes and meanings that give it some specificity. In other words, if we take the state to be not simply a matter of academic definition but as something that may or may not exist for actual people, then the ideas that make it thinkable and give it specificity should be discrete and amenable to analysis.

A brief review of the concept of the *polis* will show that there are enough differences between it and the concept of the state that it is unjustified to characterize the *polis* as a "traditional" state, "city-state," or any other kind of "state." Cornelius Castoriadis's essay "The Greek *Polis* and the Creation of Democracy" is particularly useful for such a review because of the emphasis he has placed on the shift in the meanings and functions of political forms since the time of the Greek *polis*. As Castoriadis has noted, there is no term for "state" in ancient Greek, and "the idea of a 'State' as an institution distinct and separated from the body of citizens would not have been understandable to a Greek" (Castoriadis 1991, 110).[4] This is not simply a linguistic distinction but refers to real differences in meanings and political organization. If we refer back to the social-contract metaphor (at least its Hobbesian version), we see that a basic presupposition is a presence of two distinct agencies, the people and the sovereign/state. Castoriadis argues that such a distinction cannot be found in ancient Greek thinking. His evidence is compelling, from the very direct statement by Thucydides that "*andres gar polis*" (the *polis* is the men) to the very significant mistranslation of Aristotle's *Athenaion Politeia* (properly, *The Constitution of the Athenians*) as *The Constitution of Athens* (cf. Castoriadis 1991, 81–123).[5] As

---

[3] In opposition to this traditional linking of war making and the state, Pierre Clastres has argued that war has often functioned as a defense against the formation of the state (cf. Clastres 1977).

[4] The modern Greek term for state, *kratos*, exists in ancient Greek but has a different meaning, "might" or "strength." Interestingly, it is derived from the same root as the word cancer, *karkinos*.

[5] In his translation of Plato's *Republic*, Allan Bloom argues a similar point: "The *polis* is the city, the community of men sharing a way of life and governing themselves, waging war and preserving the peace. The *polis* is the natural social group, containing all that is necessary for the development and exercise of the human powers. Today *polis* is usually translated as 'city-state'; this is done because it is recognized that a *polis* is not a state in

illustrative of this point, Castoriadis recounts the famous example of the Athenians' threat to move Athens to the west:

> For example, before the Battle of Salamis, when Themistocles has to resort to a last-ditch argument to impose his tactics, he threatens the other allied chiefs that the Athenians will take their families and their fleet and found anew their city in the West. This notwithstanding the fact that for the Athenians— even more than for the other Greeks—their land was sacred and they took pride in their claim to autochthony. (Castoriadis 1991, 109–110)

There are two major differences between *polis* and state represented here. First, there is no internal division within a *polis* between its citizens and any governing apparatus. Giddens notes: "All states—as state apparatuses—can be differentiated from the wider societies of which they are a part" (Giddens 1987, 20). The presence of a governing apparatus is central to almost all definitions of the state; the idea of a self-instituting political organization in which there is no division between governing and governed is unthinkable if we posit the state form as the model and basis for all political organizations.[6] If Castoriadis is correct, then it is not only impossible to differentiate the *polis* from the "wider society of which it is part" but it is also the case that the *polis* cannot and should not be considered a form of the state.

Second, the spatial representation of the *polis* does not depend upon an internal-external territorial dichotomy to establish its boundaries. Unlike a state, Athens does not have territoriality. From Weber's emphasis on territoriality in his definition of the state, to Wallerstein's discussion of territory in the rise of nation-states and the world system, to Deleuze and Guattari's discussion of territoriality as the spatial organization of modern politics, the presence of territorial boundaries that signify the limits (the inside and outside) of national sovereignty and "legitimate violence" or authority is everywhere taken to be a necessary and

---

the modern sense (for example, state as distinguished from society), and that the character of ancient political life was radically different from our own. However, to translate *polis* as 'city-state' implies that our notion of state is somehow contained in that of the *polis*, although only half-consciously. Hence the ancient understanding of political thinking is taken as an imperfect prefiguration of the modern one rather than as an alternative to it—an alternative alien and not adequately known to us" (Bloom 1968, 439). See also Leo Strauss (1978) for a similar argument.

[6] Poggi defines the state as "a complex set of institutional arrangements for rule operating through the continuous and regulated activities of individuals acting as occupants of offices. The state, as the sum total of such offices, reserves to itself the business of rule over a territorially bounded society; it monopolizes, in law and as far as possible in fact, all faculties and facilities pertaining to that business" (Poggi 1978, 1). See Giddens (1987, 17–26) for a discussion of common definitions of the state.

constitutive characteristic of the state. The *polis* shows us an alternative political spatiality; whereas the state is built upon a dialectic between the inside and the outside, the *polis* is only concurrent with its citizens (as Castoriadis points to with his examples of Thucydides and Themistocles) and is spatially represented by a center without limits since the scope of its autonomy and sovereignty is concurrent with the presence and movement of its only materialization, its citizens. As Poulantzas puts it:

> The space of Western Antiquity is a space with a *centre*: the *polis* (which itself has a center: the *agora*). But it has no frontiers in the modern sense of the term. It is concentric, but, having no real outside, it is also open. This centre (the *polis* and *agora*) is inscribed in a space whose essential characteristics are homogeneity and symmetry, not differentiation and hierarchy. Moreover, this geometric orientation is reproduced in the political organization of the city and the "isonomy" relationship among its citizens. . . . In this space (which is the one represented by Euclid and the Phythagoreans) people do not change their position, they simply move around. They always go to the same place, because each point in space is an exact repetition of the previous point; when they found colonies, it is only to form replicas of Athens or Rome. (Poulantzas 1978, 101)

At a minimum, Castoriadis's presentation of the *polis* as lacking territoriality and a governing apparatus separate from the citizens or society casts serious doubt on the utility and accuracy of a very large literature that has taken the state to be universal and everywhere. Moreover, it points to deeper structural differences in the ideological and institutional compositions of ancient and modern societies. For example, Castoriadis makes much of the ancient Greek separation of individual and collective interests. In modern times, at least since Hobbes, collective interests have been thought of as an accumulation of individual interests. For Hobbes, the selfish is concurrent with the moral; to act in your individual best interest is moral, rational, and the only way to produce the common good (cf. Hobbes 1962 and Macpherson 1962).[7] By contrast, the *polis* is constantly striving to eliminate the individual interest in order to secure that politics is about virtue and the building of the "good" society. As Castoriadis notes:

---

[7] Under this view, as with the market in economics, the state becomes the mechanism that transforms the multitude of self-interests into a balanced equilibrium of conflicts and compromises that defines what the "collective interest" is. Such is the pluralist view of interests and their determination of state outputs.

The same spirit is exemplified by a most striking Athenian disposition (Aristotle, *Politics*, 1330 a 20): when the *ecclesia* deliberates on matters entailing the possibility of a conflict such as a war with a neighboring *polis*, the inhabitants of the frontier zone are excluded from the vote. For they could not vote without their particular interests overwhelming their motives, while the decision must be made on general grounds only. This again shows a conception of politics diametrically opposed to the modern mentality of defense and the assertion of "interests." Interests, have, as far a possible, to be kept at bay when political decisions are made. Imagine the following disposition in the U.S. Constitution: "Whenever questions pertaining to agriculture are to be decided, senators and representatives from predominantly agricultural States cannot participate in the vote." (Castoriadis 1991, 111–112)

Indeed, there is a tension in this regard within the Constitution of the United States. A number of rules were intended to allow representatives to be as autonomous as possible from the narrow interests of their constituents. For example, the minimum population of 30,000 per representative in the House of Representatives was intended to provide a large enough pool of potential candidates so that a virtuous person could be found and so that the electorate was comprised of a large enough collection of factions so as to decrease the likelihood that a single set of interests could dominate the elections. Similarly, to have all the representatives separated from their constituents by establishing the capital in Washington, D.C., so that not a single representative would have to live among her constituents and be swayed by their interests and passions, was an attempt to secure the general over the particular.

The main difference between the ancient and the abandoned, failed, and impossible modern attempt to secure the common good is that in the case of the modern era it is assumed that citizens can abstract themselves from their own particular interests and act "as if" they were simply "public servants" and not "private citizens." We have to work to separate the representative from the citizens, but that same representative is more than capable of removing herself from her own interests. Citizens are and should be guided by self-interest; public servants, conversely, should be capable of passing judgment on these particular interests in an objective and impartial way so as to deduce what the general interest is. It is assumed that embodied in the person of George Bush are two individuals: one is selfish and replete with passions, economic interests, personal obligations, and so forth; the other is full of virtue and committed to the "common good." In other words, when Bush enters the Oval Office there is a magical transformation from private citizen to public servant, a transformation that allows for the negation of private interests within the corporate body of the state apparatuses. Interests are the stuff of "private" citizens, who are fully expected to act according to them. The same person as public servant, conversely, is an individual abstracted from material life, an individual who is most capable of being virtuous and not acting according to his own interests.

While Hobbes would obviously find such an assumption absurd, as would the ancient Greeks, the contemporary common sense does not. It does not because this assumption is founded on the same principles that produce the separation between the state apparatuses and society itself. The rise of the state is concurrent with the *abstract* split of society into the public and the private. The "public" and "private" individual is one and the same in contemporary society. When Castoriadis notes the lack of a separation between citizens and the governing apparatus in the *polis,* he is emphasizing the immediate and *concrete* position of the citizen within the political space of the *polis.* The Athenian citizen is never "private" or "public." Whereas the modern citizen is concurrently, as already noted, both private and public, the Athenian citizen is simply that, a citizen.

The use of the terms "public" and "private" thus becomes very confusing when comparing modern to premodern societies. Castoriadis seems to be aware of this in his essay on the *polis,* because when using the terms in reference to ancient Greece he initially puts them in quotation marks (cf. Castoriadis 1991, 112). Nonetheless, and in support of Hannah Arendt's (1998) arguments on the same issue, he continues to use them in order to distinguish the differences between the ancient Greek and modern forms and functions of politics and political space. A similar usage is also to be found in Habermas's work (1991). While Habermas notes that the terms "private" and "public" first appear in German in the middle of the sixteenth century and argues that no such divisions between the private and public existed in feudal societies, he goes on to argue that they did exist in ancient societies and equates the ancient Greek terms of *polis* and *oikos* with public and private (cf. Habermas 1991, ch. 1). In this sense, the categories of the public and the private are mainly functional distinctions based on different uses of space.[8] The public sphere becomes the space within which individuals can come together and discuss and formulate political opinions and positions. This is contrasted to the "state" on the one hand with its police and legal functions, and to the "private" side of civil society on the other hand with its family ties and market relations (cf. Habermas 1991, 30).[9]

The problem with defining the Athenian *polis* as a public sphere is that there is no state authority or coercive threat from above to function as the oppo-

---

[8] Raymond Geuss (2001, 12–33) demonstrates that there was a notion of privacy in the ancient world; this fits very well with the Habermasian side of things but is very far from the understanding of private implicit in the public/private split.

[9] It is to Habermas's credit that he took both the ideas and materializations of the "public sphere" seriously and his continues to be the definitive history of the rise of the spaces and functions of modern "civil society." However, we must necessarily go beyond Habermas's functionalist definitions of the public sphere in order to understand why (even in the absence of a "true" public sphere) the public/private division is so central to the intelligibility and legitimacy of the state.

site of this "civil society." Furthermore, the *oikos* (the household), although it does refer to the personal relations, properties, and so forth of the individual, need not be thought of as the opposite of the *polis* or the "public." This is particularly true since the ancient idea of citizenship is not dependent on space; one is not a "private" individual in the morning at home and then a citizen in the afternoon at the *agora*. After all, Thucydides did say that "the *polis* is the men" not that "the *polis* is an arena" or "the *polis* is the place where men go to be citizens." As further evidence of the concrete nature of citizenship, the technical/administrative offices of the *polis* were manned by slaves, not citizens. Given the necessity of equality, it was impossible to have some citizens in a position of power over fellow citizens. Castoriadis makes note of this situation:

> Characteristically, this administration, up to and including its higher echelons—police, keepers of the public archives, public finance—is composed of slaves. . . . These slaves were supervised by citizen magistrates usually drawn by lot. "Permanent bureaucracy," the task of *execution* in the strictest sense, is left to the slaves. (Castoriadis 1991, 110)

In the modern imaginary, conversely, the practice of having citizens in a position of authority over other citizens and the idea of equality are not seen as being in conflict since, as already noted, when they are functioning as a "public servant" they are acting not in their capacity as citizens but rather in their capacity as abstract individuals, as a "public" body devoid of interests and passions.

The problem here is that the modern meanings of the terms "public" and "private" are inherently tied to very modern political pathologies. The modern Greek term for private, *idioteko*, derives from the ancient Greek word for noncitizen, *idiote* (also the basis of the term *idiot*). There is a strict line separating the citizen and the *idiote*. An individual cannot be a citizen for part of the day and an *idiote* for the rest of the day. The idea of a "private citizen" or a "public *idiote*" (for lack of a better term, although the difficulty of properly phrasing this term shows the distance between the ancient and modern understandings of citizenship) is unthinkable. The citizen is, by definition, always and necessarily within common affairs, whereas the *idiote* is excluded from common affairs. It is accepted that the citizens will act according to their "private" qua individual passions, abilities, and interests. The reason that some citizens are sometimes excluded from participating in the decision-making process is precisely because they are always *concrete*; they are understood to be individuals with particular passions and interests from which it is impossible to abstract oneself.

In this sense, the division between the *idioteko* and the (again, for lack of a better term) political is always concrete in the *polis*, and for the state the division between the public and the private is always abstract. The loci of political power and sovereignty is very concrete in the Athenian *polis*: it is the citizens; not the nation, not the law, not "the people," not the general will. No po-

litical sociology is needed to identify the distribution of political power in the
polis or, for that matter, in the feudal manor. It is always concrete and readily
visible to everyone.[10]

The split of the political body into the concrete and the abstract, the
private and the public, the citizen and the public servant, is thus a constitutive
characteristic of the modern state and gives it historical specificity as a political
form. This assertion that the public-private distinction helps constitute the state
is in some ways the flip side of Althusser's argument that the state is the basis of
the public-private distinction. As Althusser puts it:

> The distinction between the public and the private is a distinc-
> tion internal to bourgeois law, and valid in the (subordinate)
> domains in which bourgeois law exercises its "authority." The
> domain of the State escapes it because the latter is "above the
> law": the State, which is the State *of* the ruling class, is neither
> public nor private; on the contrary, it is the precondition for
> any distinction between public and private. (Althusser 1971,
> 144)

Of course, this is only another way of phrasing Gramsci's famous definition of
the state as inclusive of political as well as civil society or Polanyi's argument
that the state is always present in the economic relations of bourgeois society.
What is lost in this formulation is the necessity of the appearance of the public-
private division itself. Recall Marx's discussion in the first chapter of *Capital*.
The secret behind the commodity form had been revealed already by bourgeois
political economy, labor time as the basis of exchange value. Marx's contribution was to go beyond that and show the necessity of the form itself, why the
commodity *form* was necessary for the existence of capitalism (cf. Marx 1906,
41–96). It may be the case that the likes of Gramsci, Althusser, Polanyi, and
many others have uncovered the "secret" of what lies behind the state form.
Here, I am attempting to redirect the question and uncover the basis and necessity of the form itself. For this reason, the above appropriation of Castoriadis
and his discussion of the Athenian *polis* has been focused on identifying what
distinguishes the state as a political form. The public-private division is a logical
necessity for the state in the sense that its intelligibility as a concept is founded
upon its opposition to the "civil" or "private" (the state cannot be everything and
everywhere). Moreover, and more important, since the state is a social-historical
product and not a product of definitions, we see a historical specificity of the
state form not only in terms of its particular (national) territoriality of insides

---

[10] See Göran Therborn (1976) for an analysis of how sociology arises only after the bourgeois revolutions, since before them no science was needed in order to answer questions
regarding the social loci and distribution of political power.

and outsides but also in the very peculiar division of the political body into abstract and concrete moments.

Kantorowicz as State Theorist

Ernst Kantorowicz's *The King's Two Bodies* (1957) is a text that is rarely found in contemporary discussions of state theory.[11] Nonetheless, it is perhaps the most important contribution toward a theory of the state ever written by a historian of political thought. The accomplishment of Kantorowicz is nothing less than the documentation of the institution of the state abstraction. It is Kantorowicz and the legal and ideological transformations he discusses that allow us to identify the historical point in time that gives rise to the basic abstraction of the state idea: the division between the public (abstract) and the private (concrete) body.

As Norbert Elias reminds us, the emergence of the modern state is concurrent with the transformation of the king from a feudal lord into a "public" functionary (cf. Elias 1982, 91–225). The timing of this transformation, as Elias documents it, conforms exactly with the timing of the emergence in England of the doctrine that Kantorowicz terms the "King's Two Bodies." This doctrine is nothing less than the state abstraction, the core idea that allows for the modern division of the "public" and "private" and that allows for the state to emerge as a social fact. Put simply, the "King's Two Bodies" refers to the doctrine that attributes to the king a dual existence; as a concrete person with a natural body and as an abstract person with a mystical/political body.

For Kantorowicz, the foundations of the concept of the two bodies are Christian theology and the ways legal and political theorists of the early modern era appropriated and built upon this theology. Before the King's Two Bodies concept evolves into its final, and best known, version, it is articulated in at least two earlier versions of kingship, Christ-centered and law-centered. The two bodies concept, first articulated by an anonymous cleric in Normandy around 1100 A.D., initially understood the king as a Christ-like figure, at once god and man

---

[11] There are, of course, frequent references to Kantorowicz in scholarship on medieval history and political theory. There have also been some notable appropriations of Kantorowicz in literature close to the state theory tradition. Foucault (1979, 28–31) has discussed Kantorowicz's thesis in relation to the dual status of the bodies of the condemned. Michael Rogin (1988) has used the two bodies metaphor to examine presidential self-sacrifice. There has also been much discussion of Kantorowicz's arguments in regard to the emergence of the legal fiction of the corporation (cf. Stoljar 1973). Claude Lefort (1986, 302–304) has argued that the two bodies metaphor is much more true of the ancien régime than modern societies, in that with the democratic revolutions the body politic was decapitated, and society and political power no longer could claim some sanctity or supernaturalness; this claim is addressed later on (see also Lefort 1988, 252–255). Giorgio Agamben's more recent discussion of Kantorowicz is very similar to Lefort's (cf. Agamben 1998). Closest to the appropriation of Kantorowicz attempted here is Slavoj Žižek's discussion of Kantorowicz's argument in relation to the Lacanian concept of the sublime body (Žižek 1989, 145–146 and 1991, 253–256).

(cf. Kantorowicz 1957, 42–86). This early version of the two bodies concept addressed several important questions regarding the legal and ideological status of the king in society, such as the perpetuity of kingship and the position of the king as being above the law as well as subject to the law. However, for Kantorowicz, it did not fully break with the mediaeval conception of kingship since it was primarily focused on the king's liturgical function, not political function per se. The two bodies in this respect were the physical body of the king and his divine body, which mainly functioned as a mediation between god and the people. As Kantorowicz puts it:

> The king a *gemina persona*, human by nature and divine by grace: this was the high-mediaeval equivalent of the later vision of the King's Two Bodies, and also its foreshadowing. . . . The king, by his consecration, was bound to the altar as "King" and not only—we may think of later centuries—as private person. He was "liturgical" as a king because, and in so far as, he represented and "imitated" the image of the living Christ. . . . Very naturally this Christ-imitating king was pictured and expounded also as the "mediator" between heaven and earth. (Kantorowicz 1957, 87–88)

Kantorowicz argues that a fully secularized version of the King's Two Bodies doctrine first enters political thought in the thirteenth century with Henry of Bracton (cf. Kantorowicz 1957, 143–192). Corresponding to what Kantorowicz terms "law-centered kingship," Bracton, a legal theorist, first articulated the principle that the king, although an image of god, was, like Christ with regard to Roman law, obliged to share his power with the "priests of Justice" (Kantorowicz 1957, 159–162). Rather than being sovereign by religious fiat, the king's sovereignty is now fully dependent on the law and shared with legal counsel and the courts. Having shifted the emphasis from the divine to the secular, Bracton went on the engineer the most telling and provocative innovation in the development of the King's Two Bodies doctrine. Since the divine was no longer part of the justification behind the two bodies concept, we no longer had the couplet of the physical and divine bodies. The new couplet for Bracton was based on time; one body was subject to time while the other was impervious to it. What body outside religious doctrine is impervious to time? Money. The fiscal becomes the opposite of the king's personal and particular interests and relations (which are assumed to be susceptible to time).

> This new *germinatio* of the king results from the establishment of a (so to say) extraterritorial or extrafeudal realm within the realm, an "eminent domain" the continuity of which, beyond the life of an individual king, had become a matter of public interest because the continuity and integrity of that domain were matters "that touched all." The line of distinction, there-

fore, has to be drawn between matters affecting the king alone
in his relations with individual subjects, and matters affecting
all subjects, that is, the whole polity, the community of the
realm. Better than distinguishing between the king as a private
person and the king as a nonprivate person, would be to distinguish between a king feudal and king fiscal. . . . Bracton
clearly referred to the public sphere, to "common utility"
when speaking about the Crown and the fisc. Above all, however, he attributed immutability and sempiternity not only to
church property, the *res sacrae* or (as others called them) the
res Christi, but also to the *res quasi sacrae* or *res fisci*. And
therewith there emerges that seemingly weird antithesis or
parallelism of *Christus* and *Fiscus* to which hitherto little or
no attention has been paid and which nevertheless illustrates
most accurately a central problem of political thought in the
period of transition from mediaeval to modern times. (Kantorowicz 1957, 172–173)

This innovation is fascinating because of how honest and overt it is regarding
what constitutes the "public sphere" as well as because of its indication of the
growing importance and hegemony of money capital over landed property. The
king feudal must be, at a minimum, combined with a king fiscal that is necessarily and always superior to the former, since it is money capital (and the nexus of
commodity exchange) that is now understood to be the true universal (as opposed to god or estate) "that touched all" and whose integrity must be maintained at the expense of all else. Here, Kantorowicz is acutely aware that nothing
less than the emergence of the modern state is taking place. As with Elias's assertion that the emergence of the king as a public functionary is a necessary and
critical moment in the rise of the state, Kantorowicz sees this process of the king
becoming a public functionary as being the critical moment in the transition to
our modern political forms and categories.

Whatever the angle from which we may wish to inspect the
development of English political thought, and whatever the
strand we may choose to study and isolate for this purpose,
always will the Bractonian age stand out as the most critical
period. It was then that the "community of the realm" became
conscious of the difference between the king as a personal
liege lord and the king as the supraindividual administrator of
a public sphere—a public sphere which included the fisc that
"never died" and was perpetual because no time ran against it.
(Kantorowicz 1957, 191)

By the time that the King's Two Bodies doctrine reaches its final and
most advanced form, becoming fully hegemonic in Elizabethan England, it be-

comes transformed into what Kantorowicz terms "polity-centered kingship." What makes Bracton's formulation so fascinating also makes it poor ideology; it is too overt, too honest regarding the role of the marketplace and capital. The two bodies doctrine becomes "polity" centered when the abstract body is no longer the fiscal but becomes the body politic. Shortly before this transformation of the two bodies idea, the Christian designation of *corpus mysticum* changes in ways that prefigure the changes in political and legal discourse. *Corpus mysticum* had, since and in line with the terminology of St. Paul, referred to the Eucharist (the mystical body of Christ). Around the middle of the twelfth century, Kantorowicz argues, the mysticism that had arisen around the Sacrament of the Altar was countered by the church by renaming the Eucharist *corpus Christi* (the feast of *Corpus Christi* was instituted in 1264) (Kantorowicz 1957, 194–196). This change of name signified that the Eucharist was not a representation of the body of Christ but *was* the body of Christ. Concurrently, the term *corpus mysticum* came to represent what St. Paul has originally termed *corpus Christi*, the Church qua clerical bureaucracy or collective body. Following this tendency, political theorists began to recast the two bodies doctrine so that the abstract body of the king became the political body, understood as the collective unity of the people and the administrative apparatuses. This doctrine is perhaps best summarized in the following Elizabethan legal opinion cited by Kantorowicz:

> For the King has in him Two Bodies, *viz.*, a Body natural and a Body politic. His Body natural (if it be considered in itself) is a Body mortal, subject to all Infirmities that come by Nature or Accident, to the Imbecility of Infancy or old Age, and to the like Defects that happen to the natural Bodies of other People. But his Body politic is a Body that cannot be seen or handled, consisting of Policy and Government, and constituted for the Direction of the People, and the Management of the public weal, and this Body is utterly void of Infancy, and old Age, and other natural Defects and Imbecilities. (Kantorowicz 1957, 7)

The king now becomes the head of the *corpus reipublicae mysticum* (a term that first appears in the middle of the thirteenth century), a juristic or fictitious corporate "person" qua polity (cf. Kantorowicz 1957, 207–232).

Claude Lefort has argued that the democratic revolutions (particularly the French) signify the decapitation of the political body's head (the king) and thus that the two bodies metaphor tends to correspond much more to the political reality of the ancien régime than to our own reality (Lefort 1986, 302–304).

> The democratic revolution, for so long subterranean, burst out when the body of the king was destroyed, when the body politic was decapitated and when, at the same time, the corporeality of the social was dissolved, (Lefort 1986, 303)

This reading corresponds to the view that the two bodies doctrine is primarily focused on legitimizing the king and the steady aggrandizement of royal power. This view tends to ignore the corporational character of both the body and the head. It takes the corporeality of the king too literally. Kantorowicz notes that concurrent with the shift to polity-centered kingship (this is also true of law-centered kingship in that power was shared with legal counsel) came the development of "composite authority." The king was joined by legal council and parliament as the loci of authority and power (cf. Kantorowicz 1957, 226–231). Whereas the king is a very concrete "head" of the body politic, the loci of power becomes more and more abstract as the head becomes more and more corporational. Bourgeois democratic societies simply replace "king + parliament + legal counsel" with "parliament" or "president + congress + judiciary" or any other bureaucratic ensemble. The body is the polity as a whole (the nation, the people, the public) with the state apparatuses or public servants functioning as its head. Thus, if anything, the bourgeois democratic revolutions tend to reinforce rather than subvert the two bodies doctrine.

Indeed, the rise of this doctrine is organically tied to the rise of the modern ("democratic" or not) nation-state in that the corporational unity of the "body politic" functions to establish and solidify the notion that we are not simply dealing with a group of individuals but a being or "body" somehow beyond (a sublime body) the collection of individuals. For, as Kantorowicz once more documents, the rise of the notion of the fatherland, or the national, corresponds directly with the rise of the polity-centered version of the two bodies doctrine (cf. Kantorowicz 1957, 232–272). Whereas money was the immortal body in law-centered kingship, the immortal body is now the nation/fatherland. Beyond the collection of individuals we have a sublime body, a body impervious to time and space. The individual citizen is both a materialization and a product of the "fatherland." The nation becomes a "body" composed of its citizens and the existence of the citizens, conversely, is a product of the fatherland. For Aquinas, the individual is obligated to both of his progenitors, parents and *patria* (fatherland) (cf. Kantorowicz 1957, 243). Thus, fatherland becomes concurrent with the idea of the public body. As Tolomeo of Luca noted in his continuation of Thomas Aquinas's *De Regimine Principum*, "Love for the fatherland is founded in the root of charity which puts, not the private things before those common, but the common things before the private" (Kantorowicz 1957, 242).[12]

---

[12] Of course, the idea of self-sacrifice for the greater good is directly related to the idea that it is virtuous for the individual to risk death for the greater good of the polity qua fatherland and signifies the rise of citizen armies and the movement away from the reliance on expensive and unreliable mercenaries. See Machiavelli (1962, 77–87) on the desirability of citizen armies.

The Bourgeois Foundations and Functions of the Private/Public Split

Despite its great utility for documenting the rise of the state idea, Kantorowicz's work is an inherently conservative and overly scholastic enterprise. It is an intellectual history that completely ignores the masses, the people who did or did not believe in these ideas. It completely ignores the timing of these conceptual innovations (beyond the role of innovations in religious doctrines provoking changes in political doctrines): why the rise of these ideas in early modern England (and concurrently in France, at least) and not before or after? In part, he is blinded by his argument that these ideas derive from the borrowing of religious ideas. In part, he is blinded by the belief that the object of history is great men and their ideas.

The argument here is that the two bodies doctrine, and thus the state abstraction, arises because of the transition from a barter economy to a money economy and the subsequent rise of capitalism and the bourgeoisie. The full potential of Kantorowicz's arguments can only be realized by augmenting them with the analysis of the material conditions that underpin the timing and content of these ideas. In this respect, it is striking to read *The King's Two Bodies* together with Norbert Elias's *The Civilizing Process*. In many ways, Elias and Kantorowicz are attempting to explain the same thing: how the political ideas and forms of feudalism become transformed into the nation-state. Both examine how the king and his court become "public." The great difference is that Elias places emphasis on the socioeconomic dynamics and transformations that underpin this transition.

Concurrent with the changes discussed by Kantorowicz, we see a great advancement in the centralization and consolidation of royal power. We also see a drastic increase in the use of money (depending on location, *beginning* in the eleventh or twelfth century). For Elias, this increase in the use of money is the key for explaining the rise of the king to absolutist prominence:

> The mechanism of state-formation—in the modern sense of the word state—has been shown to be, in the European area at the time when society was moving from a barter economy to a money economy, in its main outlines always the same. (Elias 1982, 98)

As the circulation of money increases, so do prices (which, under a barter economy, had tended to be very stable). The landed gentry, having a largely fixed income, experience a gradual decrease in economic power. As the economic power of the landed gentry decreases, the power of the king increases since he is able to profit from this increased circulation of money by way of taxation.[13]

---

[13] Similarly, the emerging urban bourgeoisie also becomes increasingly important and powerful.

Elias argues that this process triggers what he terms the "monopoly mecha-nism." The relatively small kingdoms of the eleventh and twelfth century (once internal power conflicts had resolved themselves and a royal court had solidi-fied) found it necessary to expand in order to keep from being subjugated by their neighbors. The need to expand reflected the relationship of territorial size to military and economic power, since the more people and resources, the more taxes, and, thus, the more military power that could be bought. The king be-comes the focus of a dual monopolization, the tendency toward the monopoliza-tion of legitimate violence and taxation. The internal competition for power within a territory results in the establishment of a monopolization of legitimate violence within the territory, which becomes the basis of the monopolization of taxation power, which results in more resources with which to gain more mili-tary power, which becomes the basis for expanding into neighboring territories, and so on.

Here we find the king of Kantorowicz's law-centered kingship, part feudal lord with the king still holding landed property, and even expanding his holdings during this time (from which rents are derived), and part public admin-istrator who levies taxes and allocates the monies for military purposes, the wages of administrators and bureaucrats, and so forth. Elias also notes the rise of what Kantorowicz terms "composite authority" in the gradual transition and differentiation of the "private" royal court into a "public" administration:

> The same picture emerges if we trace the formation of the governmental apparatus as a whole. It grows out of what might be called the "private" court and domanial administra-tion of the kings or princes. Practically all the organs of state government result from the differentiation of the functions of the royal household, sometimes with the assimilation of or-gans of autonomous local administration. When this govern-mental apparatus has finally become the public affair of the state, the household of the central ruler is at most one organ among others and finally hardly even that. (Elias 1982, 110)

With Elias, then, as with Bracton's formulations, the public/private split tends to coincide with the rise of market relations and the new role of the "king" as an administrator and fiscal manager. The rise of the bourgeoisie and its gradual inclusion within the power bloc is obviously an important influence on this process of "publicization" and the broadening of the institutional loci of author-ity (e.g., the emergence of parliament).

Elias goes beyond this point and also stresses the increasing complexity of the social division of labor and the concurrent increase in the interdependence of society (cf. Elias 1982, 164–171). This increasing differentiation is explained by Elias as a product of the money economy and the drastic increase in the func-tional complexity and interdependence of economic agents and processes. This necessitates the "civilizing process" in the sense that society must now engender the self-regulation of individual behavior (and thus the further sublimation of the drives) through, most notably but not exclusively, the institution of manners, since the actions of others are increasingly important to us and our social existence and we can no longer rely upon the simple use of force to control behavior. It also necessitates the growing rationalization and differentiation of administrative apparatuses in order to regulate and coordinate this increasingly complex nexus of social relations as well as manage the growing multitude of class antagonisms. This managing of class antagonisms becomes increasingly important as capitalism develops because the growing interdependence of social actors results in an increasing ambivalence of class interests. With the barter economy, class antagonisms and conflicts were simple:

> In societies with a barter economy there are sometimes unambiguously negative relationships, of pure, unmoderated enmity. When migrant nomads invade a settled region, there need be in their relations with the settlers no trace of mutual functional dependence. Between these groups exist pure enmity to the death. Far greater, too, in such societies, is the chance of a relationship of clear and uncomplicated mutual dependence, unmixed friendships, alliances, relations of love or service. In the peculiar black-and-white colouring of many medieval books, which often know nothing but good friends or villains, the greater susceptibility of medieval reality to relationships of this kind is clearly expressed. No doubt, at this state the chains of functional interdependence are relatively short. . . . As social functions and interests become increasingly complex and contradictory, we find more and more frequently in the behavior and feelings of people a peculiar split, a co-existence of positive and negative elements, a mixture of muted affection and muted dislike in varying proportions and nuances. The possibilities of pure, unambiguous enmity grow fewer; and, more and more perceptibly, every action taken against an opponent also threatens the social existence of its perpetrator; it disturbs the whole mechanism of chains of action of which it is a part. (Elias 1982, 168)

The increased complexity of interests necessitates new and more open governmental mechanisms for the displacement and regulation of conflict.

This observation brings us very close to the concept of relative autonomy. Poulantzas's argument that the state can only properly function as a bourgeois state if it has autonomy from the particular and narrow interests of class agents is reproduced here in the sense that the state must mediate between conflicting class interests in a way that allows for the continued existence and functioning of the bourgeois relations of production. Obviously, such a mediation of class antagonisms presupposes that no one class is completely victorious or dominating in the class struggle since the functional interdependence of social classes necessarily precludes anything like a definitive or even stable reconciliation of interests.[14]

Poulantzas's (1973) discussion of the role of the state as both a site of the displacement of social antagonisms and as the factor of cohesion for the social formation further supports this point and begs the question of the relationship between the displacement and management of antagonism and the rise of the public/private split. For, if the public/private split is concurrent with the emergence of the state (as Kantorowicz and Elias argue) that, in turn, functions to regulate and displace class antagonisms, the relationship between the class functions of the state and the curious emergence of the private/public division becomes a key issue. The role of the public/private division toward establishing a formal and juridical separation of economics and politics has been often discussed by Marxist political theorists (as already noted, and in addition to Marx's own contributions, Gramsci, Polanyi, and Althusser are particularly important in this regard).[15] But, to restate the question, why does the bourgeois separation of the political and economic take the form of the separation of the public and the private? Poulantzas's answer to this question is that by organizing the dominated classes as individual citizens, the state is able to divide the working class. Through the self-understanding of class agents as individuals qua private citizens, they are divided, disorganized and unable to properly function as a class. This is what Poulantzas, building on Marx (particularly his writings on trade unions), terms the "isolation effect":

> When Marx refers to the isolation of the economic struggle
> and contrasts it with the properly political struggle, he often
> uses the term *private* in contrast to *public*, the latter term de-
> noting the field of the political struggle. This distinction of
> private and public depends on the juridical/political, in so far
> as the agents, set up as juridico-political subjects (the private

---

[14] It is in this spirit that Bukharin (1961) discussed the role of the state as a regulator of the inherently unstable equilibrium of class interests in bourgeois society, and Gramsci discussed the organizational functions of the state: "the life of the state is conceived of as a continuous process of formation and superseding of unstable equilibria . . . between the interests of the fundamental group and the subordinate groups—equilibria in which the interests of the dominant group prevail, but only up to a certain point, i.e. stopping short of narrowly corporate economic interest" (Gramsci 1971, 182).

[15] On this issue, it is important to distinguish the public/private division from the couplet of state/civil society. Our object here is the self-organization and spontaneous understandings of society. One would be hard-pressed to find discussions framed in terms of state-civil society in the courtroom, corner coffee shop, or typical dinner table. The state-civil society division found in Hegel and continuing through the Frankfurt School to many contemporary academic circles is an analytical couplet (I will leave aside for now any discussions regarding its utility), not an artifact of society's self-understanding or the sociohistorical process that produces the state.

sphere), are opposed to the "representative" political institutions of the unity of these subjects (the public sphere). So the fact that Marx uses the category of private to mean the isolation of the economic struggle in no way implies a distinction between the private sphere of economic individuals/subjects and the political sphere; rather it indicates that the isolation of the whole series of socioeconomic relations is an effect of the juridical and the ideological. (Poulantzas 1973, 132)

The distinction between the economic and political is ideological, yet it is very real. The ideological isolation of class subjects into individuals and the concurrent organization of social life into two separate registers, one economic and the other political, is completely founded upon the public/private split. As a result of this separation, not only are the dominated classes disorganized but also the dominant classes are able, through the state, to present their interests as the interests of society as a whole, as the will of the political body.

It is no longer the king who has two bodies, everyone has two bodies. Furthermore, they are two bodies that embody the interdependency and antagonisms of the money economy as described by Elias. One body, the concrete body of the private citizen, lives within the routines and antagonisms of the everyday. The experiences of the marketplace are inherently ones of antagonism. This is the individual that one finds in Hobbes's description of the market society. Each is trying to gain at the others expenses and, in opposition to Elias's claim of the growing conflation of interests, the enemies are clear and unambiguous. There is no doubt for the concrete individual that the interests of the worker conflict with those of the boss, the tenant with those of the landlord, the consumer with those of the producer, and so on. Fernand Braudel notes this presence of stark social antagonisms during the emergence of the money economy:

> Hard cash thus found its way into everyday life by many different paths. The modern state was the great provider (taxes, mercenaries' pay in money, office-holders' salaries) and recipient of these transfers; but not the only one. Those in favorable positions sat back and received the contributions of others. And who were they? The tax collector, the salt-tax collector, the pawnbroker, the landowner, the large merchant entrepreneur and the "financier." Their net stretched everywhere. And naturally this new wealthy class, like their equivalent today, did not arouse sympathy. The faces of the financiers look down on us from the museums. On more than one occasion the painter has conveyed the ordinary man's hatred and mistrust. (Braudel 1973, 327)

Even when the "public sector" worker enters negotiations with the corresponding "public" authority, they are acting in their capacity as private qua concrete individuals. They attempt to gain as much as possible and expect the "public" bureaucracies to oppose such gains; not even the label of "public" can negate the reality that each concrete individual lives.

Even though Elias and Marx are right and capitalist society becomes more interdependent, production more socialized, this is seldom experienced as such by concrete individuals. Since all these social relationships are mediated through the commodity form, I may know that somewhere there are people laboring to produce the electricity, food, and medicine that I need to survive, but I never experience this relationship. This knowledge does me no good in my concrete existence; it helps me in no way to secure my interests and expand my life chances (unless I am a social scientist writing about such things). The social nature of my being becomes separated into another body, the body politic. This body is an abstract body, a sublime body. It is in me more than myself. Beyond my everyday material existence of eating, working, and carousing I share an existence with my fellow citizens. A common existence because it is abstracted from each concrete manifestation of existence. For this reason, Bracton's definition of the public body as the fiscal was doomed. Sure, we all know that the market impacts on all of us, that all of us have an interest in the market, but we also know that in the marketplace we are antagonistic, our interests are in conflict, we do not all share a "common" interest. The body politic becomes the receptacle of our knowledge that we are social beings, that we depend on each other for our survival, and the state becomes the mechanism through which the antagonisms of the private can be reconciled (even though only temporarily) so as to ensure the cohesion of society.

Of course, in capitalist society this search for the "common good" is doomed by the class contradictions intrinsic to it. The "public" becomes a formal and performative category. There is a disarticulation between the presumed nature of the public body and our concrete existence as private individuals. Nonetheless, people still believe in this body politic. People believe that there truly are two modes of existence, public and private, abstract and concrete. The rise of the state with its coordinating and management functions and the displacement of class contradictions to its "political" space coincides with the view that the agency of the state (a manifestation of the body politic) is a "public" one devoid of particular interests and symptomatic of our common and abstract existence. No doubt, this functions to legitimize the real (class) power and foundations of the state as well as to help cloak the true mode of our social interdependence (the nexus of social production). So far, we have done much to explain this development by way of the history of ideas and by class analysis, but why should people accept this formulation of the two bodies? What makes a doctrine that Kantorowicz termed "political theology" and that is replete with mystical overtones acceptable to the masses, especially in light of the damage this doctrine does to their class interests?

Exchange, Concrete Abstractions, and the Fetish of the Public

It should be noted that within the rise of the money economy and the growing complexity of production and economic life that Elias stresses, the social component of this process is not in the actual production or consumption of goods. In barter economies there was plenty of production and consumption; serfs produced, slaves produced, all consumed. Sure, with the increasing social and technical division of labor, the production process becomes more complex and in need of coordination. But it is, strictly speaking, not there that the increasing socialization lays. Production becomes socialized when these commodities are exchanged. In the circuit of capital, it is the point of exchange that is the loci of social interaction and coherence. I can produce as much as I like, but only when I sell my commodities am I engaged in what Alfred Sohn-Rethel (1978) terms "the social synthesis."

As we know from Marx, commodities have two values, use-value and exchange-value. As Marx also notes, exchange-value is a function of *abstract labor* while use-value is produced by *concrete labor*.

> At first sight a commodity presented itself to us as a complex of two things—use-value and exchange-value. Later on, we saw also that labour, too, possesses the same two-fold nature; for, so far as it finds expression in value, it does not possess the same characteristics that belong to it as a creator of use-values . . . the value of a commodity represents human labour in the abstract, the expenditure of human labour in general. (Marx 1906, 48)

In the circuit of capital we find the same duality of abstract and concrete that we find in the public/private split and the rise of the state abstraction. Labor comes to possess two natures, concrete and abstract. Commodities have the same dual existence, as exchange-value and use-value; use-value being always concrete since it is a function of the physical properties of the commodity and the particular needs and context of the potential user of it, and exchange-value being always abstract in that it is a function of the socially necessary labor time embodied in it (a property quite beyond the physical and concrete body of the commodity). One object, two forms of existence, abstract and concrete. Here we see a suspicious similarity to the two bodies doctrine and concurrent split of public and private.

The similarities go much deeper. Use and exchange also come to possess their own forms of presence in time; again, one concrete, the other abstract.[16] As Sohn-Rethel argues, use and exchange are mutually exclusive. One

---

[16] It is interesting to note that our modern conception of time, linear time, comes into being at this same point in historical time. Linear time is inherently abstract in that it is abstracted from the concrete and particular events that may occur in nature and society.

cannot exchange and use at the same time. Imagine a grocer who drinks from a milk bottle on the shelf and then keeps it there to sell. Or consider the common practice of merchants providing "demonstration" models (as with cars, electronics, etc.) so as to maintain the exchange integrity of the actual commodity that will change ownership. Use violates the sociotemporal requisites of exchange. According to Sohn-Rethel, this leads to an abstract and denatured presence of commodities in time:

> There, in the market place and in shop windows, things stand still. They are under the spell of one activity only; to change owners. They stand there waiting to be sold. While they are there for exchange they are not there for use. A commodity marked out at a definite price, for instance, is looked upon as being frozen to absolute immutability throughout the time during which its price remains unaltered. And the spell does not only bind the doings of man. Even nature herself is supposed to abstain from any ravages of the body of this commodity and to hold her breath, as it were, for the sake of this social business of man. Evidently, even the aspect of nonhuman nature is affected by the banishment of use from the sphere of exchange. (Sohn-Rethel 1978, 25)

Sohn-Rethel's great contribution to this area of inquiry is his discovery that the abstraction that takes place during this time of exchange is not an abstraction in thought but an abstraction in action, a "concrete abstraction." When we go to the market to purchase a commodity, our minds are filled with thoughts of utility. We will check the expiration date on the milk, flip through the pages of a book, smell and squeeze the fruits and vegetables, try on the clothes, etc. Nonetheless, the action of exchange itself, the participation in the social nexus of interdependence, is necessarily abstracted from use and the realm of the concrete. "In exchange, *the action is social, the minds are private*" (Sohn-Rethel 1978, 29). The mode of social interaction and interdependence proper to capitalist society is abstract even before it becomes detached from social activity and becomes cast as the equally abstract body politic.

Money becomes a key element in this process. The term "money economy" takes on deeper significance once we consider the abstraction proper to money and exchange itself. On one level, money also embodies this abstraction of exchange value. Money has a concrete materiality: so much silver or copper or paper and ink. But its value in exchange is obviously not a property of this

---

This is opposed to the circular time (Henri Lefebvre) or task-oriented time (E. P. Thompson) of precapitalist societies, a time that is inherently concrete because it corresponds directly to the occurrence and duration of an event: the time of harvest, of high tide, of the frying of an egg, of the saying of a prayer, etc. (cf. Thompson 1967 and Lefebvre 1991).

materiality (at least not most of the time). Since money is only an object of exchange and not of use, its materiality is also abstracted from time and its effects:

> A coin, therefore, is a thing which conforms to the exchange abstraction and is supposed, among other things, to consist of an immutable substance, a substance over which time has no power, and which stands in antithetic contrast to any matter found in nature. (Sohn-Rethel 1978, 59)

Money is a sublime body; it possesses properties that are beyond its material composition. Even though we know that the substance of money is not supernatural we act "as if" it were; we act "as if" time has no effect on the materiality of money. Moreover, and here we have the most acute form of a concrete abstraction, at the time of exchange, when we hand over our coins for a commodity, we are establishing a relation of equivalence. We know that the coins and commodity are not equal on the concrete level of use, indeed it is precisely for this reason that we exchange them. Nonetheless, our actions say the opposite; they say that they are equal, that one apple = one dollar. It is not in our minds that this abstraction occurs but in our actions. The abstraction of exchange as a concrete abstraction provides us with the everyday life prefiguration and foundation of the conceptual abstraction of the public/private split.

The apparently strange, mystical, "theological" doctrine that Kantorowicz describes becomes very rational once we understand that this duality of existence, this assertion that the same body has two modes of existence, one concrete the other abstract, is established and reasserted every time we participate in commodity exchange. The rise of the money economy not only produces the class agents and political and economic needs that help explain the rise of the two bodies doctrine and the public/private split, but also engenders social practices that lay the foundation for the belief in these ideas by the population as a whole. We first establish the two bodies doctrine in practice and then we come to accept it in our consciousness. Moreover, this duality of the concrete and abstract comes to characterize more than just commodities and the social body. Production comes to take on the same form with the separation of productive and unproductive labor and intellectual and manual labor. Even capital is separated into productive and finance capital.

Finally we have reached the point where the phrase "fetish of the public" can be understood. The striking parallel between the development of our modern categories of the public and private that founds the state and the categories intrinsic to the exchange of commodities also extends to the question of fetishism. As is well known, the commodity fetish involves the ascription of social qualities to inanimate objects, commodities. Because of the mediation of the commodity form, we misrecognize our social interactions as being interactions with things and not other people. Of course, we do know that we are involved in social relationships during exchange and that there are real people who produce the commodities that we consume and that there are real people who consume the commodities we produce. As has already been pointed out, though, the loci of the fetish are not so much on the level of consciousness as they are on the level of practice. The fetish is the act whereby we treat something "as if" it is not what it actually is. We act "as if" time has no effect on the commodity during the time of exchange although we know that it does. We act "as if" money was made of sublime supernatural materials even though we know that it is not. We know that the apple and the dollar bill are not the same, but nonetheless we act "as if" they were. We act "as if" commodities existed by their own efficacy, "as if" they were not the product of concrete labor, because the abstracted time of the point of exchange demands that we act only on the level of exchange value.

The public-private division becomes acted out in a similar way. We know the king only has one body, we know that the wealthy have an inordinate influence on "public" policy, we know that we too have only one body, and we act "as if" we did not know. The reification that takes place is that the social synthesis function of exchange becomes reified as the body politic. This reification takes the form, out of necessity, of rearticulating our social interconnectedness as a property of the state qua body politic ("the public") rather than as the property of the totality of "private" social activities that find their realization and social character in the web of exchange. It is this "private" arena that produces all those conflicts and contradictions that Elias and Poulantzas (as well as Marx, Bukharin, Gramsci, and many more) identified as the major reason behind the need for a state that functions to organize the increasingly complex production process and to manage and control ever-increasing and complex social antagonisms. The social nature of man in this context is to be found in his social being, in the interconnectedness of our activities within the routines of our everyday life, in the sharing of place and time.[17] What is not social, or at least not common, is our interests. The deep contradictions and fissures of interests are what threaten to dissolve this nexus of social relations. For this reason, the question of interests becomes deformed by the state. The political body asserts that what unites us are interests, the "general will," "common good," or some other version of this idea of universality on the level of interests. The formal separation of the economic and the political takes this form, then, of distinction between the particular and the universal. But what are these interests? For sure, they cannot be found in the arena of the "private." They are abstract interests, interests that are beyond our existence as concrete individuals living in a capitalist society

---

[17] Of course, the ancient Athenians were very conscious of this. It is the sharing of place and the mobilization of human agency toward improving our existence in this place that defines our social, or political (it is the same, after all, for Aristotle), nature. The question of interest is a different matter. There is no "general will," "public interest," or any other such dubious abstraction in the political thought of the *polis*. Interests are always concrete and always, albeit to varying degrees, antagonistic. The common, as illustrated in the discussion of Castoriadis earlier, refers to the people's existence as a *polis* and coparticipation in politics; the common is not to be found in interest.

(our private body) and to be found in our other body (the abstract body of the "body politic"). The idea of the body politic becomes the necessary fantasy that supports the reality of our concrete existence by providing an imaginary and harmonious unity of individuals to support their antagonistic unity in the nexus of the relations of production.[18]

Thus, the establishment of the body politic is founded on a series of fetishizing acts that produce the "public." If the state/body politic is to exist, we must act "as if" there actually were universal interests, that the machinery of the state really does represent "us" and functions to secure these interests of the "nation" or "people." How is this accomplished? It is accomplished by creating a whole series of activities that mimic the social synthesis: the institution of universal suffrage, the replacement of privilege with universal rights, the institution of the priests of politics as representatives of the will of the people, and, not unimportantly, through the constitution of a shared identity and sense of being as political community (a process examined in much greater detail in Chapters 4 and 5). In other words, a series of activities is created that treats concrete individuals "as if" all were the same; "as if" we could abstract from each determinate/concrete body a sublime body that unites them in their difference.

These developments do not produce a social synthesis but only present it as a pure formality, a matter of definition and shared sentiment. This fetish of the public and its corresponding dismemberment of the political from the non-political (as Lefebvre says, concurrently fictitious and real, cohesive through its incoherence) contains within it what can only ultimately be an unsatisfactory vision of social unity since it is precisely what is not common in our social existence that is presented as the common. "The public" ultimately leads us to abstract individualism by emptying from us all the particular determinations that make us concrete individuals.

Let us take as a symptomatic example of this development the divergent forms of situation comedies and soap operas. With situation comedies, we find that almost all of the successful examples of this genre, from *The Honeymooners* and *I Love Lucy* to *Gilligan's Island, The Odd Couple, All in the Family, M*A*S*H, Cheers, Seinfeld*, and *Friends*, involve a shared, social, determinate, concrete existence. Whether taking place in a New York City apartment building (as most do) or a bar, island, or military base, we have an ensemble of determinate individuals sharing their existence by occupying the same spaces and temporal rhythms. What is lacking is the existence of the abstract isolation brought about by this "pure formality" and its modern spatial form, suburbia (where we live "as if" we did not live in a community by retreating into separate spaces of living and movement so that, by way of our cars and detached houses with high fences, we can minimize any interactions with those who may happen to live around us). Furthermore, the conflicts presented in these comedies are

---

[18] This point dovetails with the Lacanian argument that fantasy is not some dreamlike illusion but precisely that which gives coherence and consistency to reality. See Žižek (1997, ch.1) for a discussion of the Lacanian concept of fantasy.

always conflicts of temperament and vision; conflicts over what movie to see, the goodness or badness of segregation/war/monogamy/chauvinism/etc., how to deal with an annoying neighbor or roommate, what the proper gift is for a particular occasion, the best way to get rich quick, how to cajole your spouse or friend into accepting your vision of the good. There are many possible scenarios; the point is that in these communal spaces the conflicts of interest are always absent. These are conflicts of opinion and appetite, but, by and large, the group is working together in search of happiness. The well-being of one does not detract from the well-being of the other; just the opposite, the well-being of each individual is a function of the well-being and success of the collective. Soap operas are exactly the opposite. They take place in suburbia (usually, Long Island or California), in large detached houses, and the conflicts that take place are always conflicts of interest: kidnappings, corporate takeovers, love triangles, sibling rivalries, racketeering, murder. In almost all cases, the well-being of one individual hinges on the misery of another.

Why do comedy and drama take these forms in contemporary popular culture? We find that, on the one hand, the success of soap operas relies upon the identification of the viewer with the characters themselves. To identify with the villain and the pleasure he takes by extending his interests at the expense of others and/or to identify with the less powerful (always honest and ethical) and either feel outrage at the injustice that always seems to befall the good or, at times, delight when they are actually able to thwart the villains. In other words, in order to engender our identification with the characters and involve us in the emotional roller coaster of the surprises and unfolding of events, the characters are made concrete; soap operas mimic our antagonistic experiences as individuals competing in the marketplace by creating this very familiar context of concrete individuals engaged in conflicts of interests.[19] Comedies do not rely upon any identification of the viewer with the characters. Our shared/concrete existence in place and time is not a reflection of egotistic qualities but, rather, our communal attributes. Thus, by creating a situation where we are not likely to identify with any particular character (since such an ideal existence, one devoid of conflict of interest, is something we may long for but seldom experience, and in this sense the characters are so concrete and tied to place that we have no way of identifying with them), the communal situation becomes the focus of the show. In order to create delight and ease, the commonality of space and activity is reflected back to us as exactly that which we know it to be, the authentic and truly common. Furthermore, our desire for a life devoid of social alienation is

---

[19] This is further evidenced by the large list of publications that focus on the individual characters in these shows and inform the viewers of what they are "really" like and what can be expected of these characters in the future. Beyond publications that deal with the usual infatuation with celebrity, there are no such publications that describe the characters in situation comedies.

drawn upon to attract us to the setting itself.[20] As drawn as we may be to these desirable settings (where even life as a prisoner of war is fun and harmonious), this non-antagonistic reality is shown to us in the only way it can exist in bourgeois society: as farce. Soap operas are the cultural residue of our "private" lives, an existence full of angst and conflict, while situation comedies become the cultural expression of our desired form of "public" existence, a nonformal and concrete public existence that can now only exist as farce.[21]

There are surely many more examples of popular culture that refract back to us the pathologies and tensions inherent in the public/private split. But this tension and its performative dimension is perhaps nowhere better illustrated than in the many contemporary examples of political corruption. The magical transformation from private citizen to public servant (the two bodies doctrine at its most visible) noted earlier is everywhere dependent upon the type of fetishizing practices that result in this fetish of the public. The analysis of political corruption in the following chapter identifies one ensemble of practices that support the fiction of state apparatuses as separated from the particular interests of "private" life and manned by individuals who are abstracted from their material existence and are able to function in an objective and impartial way with regard to concrete social interests. The historical rise of the discourse on political corruption is nothing less than the attempt to establish the boundaries between what constitutes a normal presence of the private within the "abstract" body of the public and what constitutes a pathological presence. Given our knowledge that everywhere individuals have only a singular and concrete existence, bourgeois society must produce a set of conditions where we are led to act "as if" this were not the case. The language of corruption has had the historical effect of creating a large and legally regulated series of practices that legitimize the unavoidable and systemic presence of private interests in the "body politic" by treating only some forms of this presence as being a subversion of the public by the private. The rigor with which the state polices its personnel and demands allegiance to the fiction of the public fetish by compelling this personnel to act "as if" they were abstract individuals illustrates both the impossibility of a true public (of a real universality of interests) and the constant threat that this impossibility poses to the existence and legitimacy of the state.

---

[20] This desire is perfectly expressed in the theme song of *Cheers*, a place where everyone knows your name and are always glad that you came.

[21] The danger posed by the environmentalist movement to modern politics is exactly on this level. By concretizing the universality of social being in terms of time and place, it threatens to subvert the modern political structure of abstract individualism by replacing it with a concrete universal through which individuals can organize and think their relations with others.

3

Political Corruption as Symptom of the Public Fetish; or, Rules of Separation and Illusions of Purity in Bourgeois Societies

What's breaking into a bank compared with founding a bank?
—Bertolt Brecht, *The Threepenny Opera*

Defilement is never an isolated event. It cannot occur except in view of a systematic ordering of ideas. Hence any piece-meal interpretation of pollution rules of another culture is bound to fail. For the only way in which pollution ideas make sense is in reference to a total structure of thought whose keystone, boundaries, margins and internal lines are held in relation by rituals of separation.
—Mary Douglas, *Purity and Danger*

What Is Political Corruption?

The split of society into the public and the private brings with it the immense task of constantly reproducing and legitimizing this split. As argued in the previous chapter, the material foundations for the split can be found in everyday life; notably, the exchange of commodities. This is not enough. It may be a necessary condition and one that helps to explain the propensity of people to believe in the idea of two bodies, one public and one private, but it is not a sufficient condition. As already noted, the rise of capitalism and its impact on the class structures and struggles of society does a good deal to explain the public/private split as does the articulation of these struggles in political and legal theory. The articulations of this split in the theories that Kantorowicz discusses provide a telling indication of how the public/private division was first instituted and entered political discourse. However, these theoretical developments possess no agency in the reproduction of the fetishism of the public. The concepts and legal precedents that accompany the public/private split have long been established (at

51

least in advanced capitalist societies) and have replaced the political and legal doctrines of feudalism. The challenge that the public/private split faces today is much more severe than the threat that the antiquated ideas of feudalism ever posed. The public/private split must contend with the constant threat that its fetishistic nature, that the real impossibility of the public, will be exposed and that the entire conceptual framework that supports the state and capitalist productive relations will collapse.

In this regard, the discourse surrounding the phenomenon of "political corruption" is particularly important for understanding the presence of the two bodies doctrine in modern politics and for disclosing how some of the short circuits inevitable in the public/private split are mediated. Almost all modern definitions of political corruption tend to emphasize the subversion of the public good by private interests. Among the more famous definitions of corruption, Joseph Nye has defined it as "behavior which deviates from the formal duties of a public role because of private-regarding (personal, close family, private clique) pecuniary or state gains; or violates rules against the exercise of certain types of private-regarding influence" (Nye 1989, 966). Similarly, Carl Friedrich has argued that

> Corruption is a kind of behavior which deviates from the norm actually prevalent or believed to prevail in a given context, such as the political. It is deviant behavior associated with a particular motivation, namely that of private gain at public expense. But whether this was the motivation or not, it is the fact that private gain was secured at public expense that matters. Such private gain may be a monetary one, and in the minds of the general public it usually is, but it may take other forms. (Friedrich 1989, 15)[1]

The relevancy of the concept of corruption to the question of the public/private split is apparent. Contained within the modern understanding of corruption are two interrelated assumptions: that mutually exclusive public and private interests exist and that public servants must necessarily abstract themselves from the realm of the private in order to properly function.

The significance and relative historical novelty of this definition has been ignored in the contemporary literature on political corruption. The tendency has been to emphasize the continuity of the concept of political corruption from the ancient to modern times. Carl Friedrich has argued that the basic un-

---

[1] For a discussion of the various ways that political corruption has been defined, see Heidenheimer, Johnston, and LeVine (1989). They argue that there are three ways that corruption has been defined: "public office centered," as a deviation from the requisites of public office, "market centered," as rent-seeking activity by civil servants, and "public interest centered," as action that does damage to the public interest. All three of these forms of definition contain the idea that the public is subverted by the private.

derstanding of corruption as, "a general disease of the body politic" (Friedrich 1989, 18), is common to the ancients and the moderns. John Noonan (1984) has argued that the category of bribery, the most obvious form of political corruption, goes back at least to the fifteenth century B.C. and that the history of the concept is an ever-increasing realization and materialization of the need for public officials to put aside their private interests and strive for the public weal:

> The notion of fidelity in office, as old as Cicero, is inextricably bound to the concept of public interest distinct from private advantage. It is beyond debate that officials of the government are relied upon to act for the public interest distinct from private advantage. (Noonan 1984, 704)

Similarly, there are usually numerous references to Plato, Aristotle, and Machiavelli when tracing the history of the concept of corruption. Aristotle is often cited for his assertion that political forms can be corrupted. In Aristotle's classification of the three kinds of constitution, he lists kingship, aristocracy, and polity.[2] He goes on to note that each can be corrupted. His discussion of kingship is particularly relevant, because what constitutes the corruption of kinship into tyranny is the disregard the tyrant has for his subjects: he rules only to further his own "interests" (cf. Aristotle 1958, 373–375). Machiavelli's discussion of the function and causes of corruption is also often discussed, especially as he developed them in *The Discourses* regarding the decline of the republic of Rome (cf. Machiavelli 1970, esp. book 1). Sara Shumer has noted that inclusive in Machiavelli's discussion of corruption is the idea of the subversion of the public by the private:

> One dimension of political corruption is the privatization both of the average citizen and those in office. In the corrupt state, men locate their values wholly within the private sphere and they use the public sphere to promote private interests. (Shumer 1979, 9)

One obvious effect of this approach is to project back throughout history the modern categories of the private and public. Friedrich's ascribing the metaphors of "political body" and "disease" to ancient conceptions is quite telling, especially in light of Kantorowicz's meticulous documentation of the rise of the idea of the political body almost two millennia after Plato and Aristotle. The apparent lack of a word for bribery in ancient Greek also presents a problem for those who assume an unbroken line in the concept of corruption. Mark Philp

---

[2] Aristotle sometimes identifies four types of constitution, adding oligarchy to the list above and replacing polity with democracy. In the section of the *Ethics* where he discusses corruption, he lists only three types of constitution.

notes that there are many words in ancient Greek that make no distinction between a gift and a bribe (*doron, lemma, chresmasi peithein*) since, for the
Greeks, to persuade through gift giving was acceptable and no perversion of
judgment could be assumed (Philp 1997, 26). He makes the point that if the
Greeks have no conception of bribery, then this puts into question the whole
idea of a public body in ancient Greece:

> If these were the only terms for bribery in the Ancient Greek
> world we would have to take the view that there is a basic un-
> translatability of the terms between us and them—that they not
> only failed to distinguish gifts and bribes, but that they also
> had no real concept of public office or trust. (Philp 1997, 26)

He is absolutely right. He goes on to argue, following Harvey (1985), that there
was a term for bribery in ancient Greece, *diaphtheirein*.[3] However, in opposition
to Philp's interpretation, it is not true that *diaphtheirein* has the same status as
the modern term *bribery* or that it can be said to constitute a form of corruption
in the modern sense. *Diaphtheirein* refers to corrosion and destruction, to the
reduction of the capacity to make proper decisions and the ability to do good.
All bribery is not corruption in the modern sense. A closer reading of Harvey's
discussion of *diaphtheirein* reveals this point. Harvey takes great pains to show
that, in contrast to and concurrent with neutral and positive terms, there did indeed exist at least one negative term (*diaphtheirein*) for influencing through
giving money and gifts. Nowhere, however, do we find any reference to "public
trust," "private interest," or any such category we usually use in discussing bribery and corruption. Bribery as *diaphtheirein* was negative because it implied that
the citizen, by way of accepting a bribe, was no longer able to properly act as a
citizen since his will and power to judge had been destroyed. As Harvey puts it:

> The man who takes a bribe surrenders his free will; what he
> says and does he does for another, and in that sense he no
> longer exists as an independent individual: he is a nonentity.
> That, I suggest, is the essential point. (Harvey 1985, 86)

Rather than some "public trust" succumbing to "private interests," the recipient
of a "bribe" has lost the ability to be a citizen by relinquishing his autonomy.
Like slaves, merchants, and women, all precluded from being citizens since they
all lacked basic requisites for properly acting as a citizen, so the recipient of a
bribe is incapable of the autonomous thought and moral judgment necessary for
being a citizen.

---

[3] It is quite telling that the possibility that there was no conception of "public office or
trust" in ancient Greece is seen as so preposterous that it is taken as a sure sign that they
must have had some concept of bribery.

In line with the argument of the previous chapter that the categories of the public and private emerge only in the early modern period and not before, so too our modern concept of corruption could not exist before. Bribery in ancient Greece is but one example of the incongruity of our modern political ideas with precapitalist realities. Even up to Machiavelli, in contrast to the argument by Shumer noted above, our modern concept of corruption seems to be lacking. Albert Hirschman's *The Passions and the Interests* is particularly useful for this line of questioning. In addition to the argument regarding the rise of the public and the private, we also have the question of the rise of the concept of interests. For Hirschman, it is only in the modern era that the concept of interests emerges, and this marks a radical break with premodern conceptions of the good. Very much in agreement with the argument in the previous chapter that the rise of the money economy and the bourgeoisie engender a new political vocabulary and organizational forms, for Hirschman it is the increasing dominance of finance and money that explains the change in the term "interest" from being simply a financial term to a concept that is central to our understanding and organization of contemporary politics (cf. Hirschman 1977).[4] It is in this context that Hirschman sheds light on the question of Machiavelli's notion of corruption and notes how the term corruption went through a similar transformation in meaning as interest:

> "Corruption" has a similar semantic trajectory. In the writings of Machiavelli, who took the term from Polybius, *corruzione* stood for deterioration in the quality of government, no matter for what reason it may occur. The term was still used with this inclusive meaning in eighteenth-century England, although it became also identified with bribery at that time. Eventually the monetary meaning drove the nonmonetary one out almost completely (Hirschman 1977, 40).[5]

---

[4] Marcel Mauss's *The Gift* is also relevant to this question: "The very word 'interest' is itself recent, originally an accounting technique: the Latin word *interest* was written on account books against the sums of interest that had to be collected. In ancient systems of morality of the most epicurean kind it is the good and pleasurable that is sought after, and not material utility. The victory of rationalism and mercantilism was needed before the notions of profit and the individual, raised to the level of principles, were introduced. One can almost date—since Mandeville's *The Fable of the Bees*—the triumph of the notion of individual interest. Only with great difficulty and the use of periphrasis can these two words be translated into Latin, Greek, or Arabic" (Mauss 1990, 76). See also Louis Dumont (1977) on the rise of these ideas.

[5] The question of corruption is particularly confusing in the case of Machiavelli because already present in his work is the public/private split and the question of interests, as when he states that "the senators sent two ambassadors to beg him to set aside private enmities, and in the public interest to make the nomination" (Machiavelli 1970, 523). In this context, it is easy to accept Schumer's argument that the subversion of the public by the private is one dimension of corruption for Machiavelli. But, even if we accept this

The Greek term of *diaphtheirein* and the Latin term of *corruzione*, in spite of their usual translation as corruption, refer to an understanding of corruption that is quite foreign to our modern one. In this sense, political corruption is an exclusively modern phenomenon made possible only after the rise of the public/private split and the concept of interests. Although it may be quite impossible, and not particularly important from the perspective of the present work, to provide some specific date or event that signals the moment that our modern concept of corruption emerges, it is appropriate to locate it within the general processes discussed in the previous chapter and claim that our modern understanding of corruption becomes possible and thinkable as capitalism and the state emerge and become dominant.[6]

Why Corruption?

To note the novelty of the modern concept of political corruption and to note the basic preconditions of its existence beg the question of why the term corruption came to represent the idea of the subversion of the public interest by private interests. This is even more the case when one notes deeper differences in meaning between the two concepts of corruption. In the traditional understanding of

---

argument, Hirschman is still correct in his assessment, and the concept of corruption found in Machiavelli is still very much traditional because private interests in this context function as bribery did in the earlier example, as something that decreases virtue. Thus, private interests are bad *in themselves*, and corruption is not simply the improper presence of private interests within the public. For example, the idea Schumer puts forth that average citizens are corrupted by their privatization is completely unthinkable from the point of view of the modern understanding of corruption. It does not make sense in the modern context to say, for example, that voters are corrupt because they vote according to their private interests. In fact, it is never possible to say that "private" citizens are ever corrupt in the modern sense of the term (although they can certainly be corrupting, as when they tempt public officials with bribes and favors). This difference between the traditional and the modern understanding of corruption is further examined in the next section.

[6] Given that the modern concept of corruption becomes thinkable at any point after the rise of the public/private split, it seems possible, in opposition to both Mauss and Hirschman, that the modern use of the term occurs well before either Mandeville (Mauss's argument; *The Fable of the Bees* was published in 1714 with the very revealing subtitle *Private Vices, Publick Benefits*) or the late eighteenth/early nineteenth centuries (Hirschman's argument). For example, Francis Bacon was convicted of political corruption qua bribery in 1621. He famously confessed, "I am guilty of corruption and do renounce all defense." Given the dominance of the two bodies doctrine in Elizabethan England and the relative novelty of convicting a judge for bribery (at that time, it was common for judges to receive gifts from winning parties) it seems very likely that already with Bacon we have the use of the term of corruption in the modern sense. The important point here is that the rise of the modern concept of corruption should not be thought of as an event but, rather, as a process that begins with the rise of the two bodies doctrine and becomes fully realized by the time of the bourgeois revolutions.

corruption, there was a strong imagery of decay and regression, of something becoming less and less capable, potent, or virtuous. The idea that through disease, old age, the influence of vice, or any other reason, the ability to seek the good and virtuous is decreased/destroyed. Here, we have the corruption of the mind, morals, and the will. The term still retains this meaning today; we completely understand the use of the term in the claim, for example, that the youth of Athens were corrupted by Socrates, and we use the term in essentially the same way when we claim that the minds of the young are corrupted by the entertainment industry or that the ability to make sound decisions is corrupted by religious cults, various psychological disorders, and so on. What is interesting here is that there is a clear division of good and bad; vice is never good nor is disease or psychosis.

By contrast, in the modern understanding of corruption there is not a division based on something that in itself is good and desirable and something that is not. Private interests are not bad. Quite the opposite, the whole line of questioning from Weber's *The Protestant Work Ethic and the Spirit of Capitalism* to Hirschman's *The Passions and the Interests* has been focused on explaining how private interests, particularly in the economistic sense, came to be welcomed as something positive.[7] How then can two things, public and private interests, that are in themselves seen as proper and good come to constitute something that is bad and improper? Mary Douglas does much to answer this question when she notes that notions of purity and cleanliness have nothing to do with something that in itself is dirty. For Douglas, dirt is best understood as something that is out of place:

> Shoes are not dirty in themselves, but it is dirty to place them on the dining table; food is not dirty in itself, but it is dirty to leave cooking utensils in the bedroom, or food bespattered on clothing; similarly, bathroom equipment in the drawing room; clothes lying on chairs; outdoor things indoors; upstairs things downstairs; underclothing appearing where overclothing should be, and so on. In short, our pollution behaviour is the reaction which condemns any object or idea likely to confuse cherished classifications. (Douglas 1966, 36–37)

Private interests and public interests are both perfectly fine, as long as they stay in their proper places. Once we have the contamination of the public by the private, politicians and politics itself become dirty, tainted, infected, and thus cor-

---

[7] Even in famous Federalist Paper #10, faction is not something bad in and of itself or something that can be avoided without eliminating political freedom. Only when a faction represents a majority and is able to violate the rights of a minority are private interests seen as resulting in bad political actions. More overtly, Federalist Paper #51 explicitly argues that each branch and institution of government acting in its own self-interest is necessary for the production of the public good since only ambition can counter ambition.

rupt. The opposite is equally true; once we have an invasion of the private by the public (for example, public authorities being able to regulate "private" behaviors such as sexual, religious, and so forth) we come to equally negative conclusions regarding the transgression of the categorical separation of private and public. The modern notion of political corruption is thus much closer to the idea of corruption as adulteration rather than as deterioration of the capacity for the good. This idea of political corruption is consistent with the use of corruption to describe the loss of the purity of one substance by the introduction of another: the way that wine can be corrupted by water or a flowerbed can be corrupted by weeds.

To further emphasize these differences in meaning, let us take as an illustrative example the likely possibility that Ronald Reagan had Alzheimer's disease in the later years of his presidency. Assuming that it had progressed to the point of hindering his ability to reason and make decisions, this would constitute corruption in the classical sense in the same way that bribery constituted corruption—his capacity to think and act in an autonomous and rational way was diminished. It is obviously not corruption in the modern sense since there is no instance of the contamination of the public interest by private interests. The Clinton coffee scandals, where prospective campaign contributors were invited to coffees at the White House, are an example of the opposite. It is hard to imagine that drinking coffee could ever result in corruption in the traditional sense (unless one became so addicted to it that the ability to reason was lost, one had to resort to crime in order to support the consumption of coffee, and so forth), but it can easily result in corruption in the modern sense. If that coffee is being consumed by prospective campaign contributors in a "public" area, the nonresidential areas of the White House, it can be said to constitute political corruption because the president is allowing his private interests to contaminate the purity of the public. This space within the White House is not "public" simply because it is owned by "the public" but rather because it is there for his use as a public servant and not as a private citizen. If coffee is being consumed and contributions being sought in space that is for the president's use as a private individual, no corruption is present. The same people, the same coffee, the same money changing hands, the only difference being the room it is occurring within is all the difference between corruption and noncorruption.

In light of these stark differences, how is it possible that the modern and traditional ideas of corruption are so easily conflated and confused? Although the meanings are very different, both understandings of political corruption attempt to establish a normative distinction between what is desirable and what is not. In the traditional understanding of political corruption, the characteristics of a citizen, king, or regime as they *should* be are established and contrasted with those characteristics that are seen as bad/undesirable from the point of view of that desired reality. In the modern understanding, a strict division of the public and private is asserted, and various phenomena that may conflict with that presumed division are termed corruption. This difference between what should be and keeping things in their "proper" place is immensely significant.

On the one hand we have a normative political project that posits what the good is and on this basis is able to establish what is corrupt/bad. On the other hand we have the desirable/undesirable distinction established in a more technocratic and underhanded way. The proper ordering of all social things is posited in the form of ontological assumptions regarding the public/private; phenomena that pose a challenge to this vision of how things are become branded as corrupt.

Since the modern concept of corruption does not function as an explicitly normative construct but rather as an articulation of categories of bourgeois political ontology, it has the effect of constituting and reaffirming the dominant public/private split through its application and subsequent categorization of phenomena as corrupt or uncorrupt, as normal and pathological. In so doing, the normative dimension of the modern concept of corruption becomes manifest precisely because of its way of categorizing social phenomenon. By establishing the division between the normal and pathological in the public/private split, the modern understanding of political corruption is at once making a statement of fact and presenting us with the political goal of fully realizing the "normal." As Georges Canguilhem notes in his discussion of the foundations of the concept of the normal:

> In the discussion of these meanings [of normal] it has been pointed out how ambiguous this term is since it designates at once a fact and "a value attributed to this fact by the person speaking, by virtue of an evaluative judgment for which he takes responsibility." One should also stress how this ambiguity is deepened by the realist philosophical tradition which holds that, as every generality is the sign of an essence, and every perfection the realization of the essence, a generality observable in fact takes the value of realized perfection, and a common characteristic, the value of an ideal type. (Canguilhem 1991, 125)

In this way, the modern concept of corruption repeats the normative/political emphasis of the traditional understanding of political corruption but does so in an essentialist and apolitical way. The confusion of the two concepts of political corruption thus appears to be, at least partly, a result of the similar normative function of situating what is politically desirable and what is not. But, nonetheless, already built into the modern concept of corruption is an ahistorical and acritical understanding of political phenomena that takes the integrity of the public/private split at face value, as a quality immanent in all societies, as the normal. For this reason, it is rare that the historical specificity and social embeddedness of the concept of political corruption becomes visible to observers. Similarly, by conflating the two concepts of corruption, the reception of the modern concept of corruption reifies it back throughout history and gives the public/private split the appearance of the eternal.

Characteristically, most contemporary discussions of political corruption within political science occur within the subfield of comparative politics, not political theory. Under the guise of discussions on clientelism, patronage, totalitarianism, civil society, and so forth, comparative politics has spent much of its time demonstrating the normalcy of the United States and other advanced capitalist societies by demonstrating the pathologies of "less developed" nations.[8] Very much in line with the comments by Canguilhem quoted above, an omnipresent assumption in this literature is that the public and private are essential attributes of human societies and that political development and advancement entails the realization of this fact and the formation of institutions, laws, and attitudes that end the systematic corruption prevalent in these underdeveloped societies. The following quote from Jacob van Klavern is typical:

> We know that the political systems of the so-called underdeveloped regions still remain in the stage of systematic corruption, and there are good reasons for this which we cannot go into here. For simplicity's sake, let us say that the Age of Enlightenment has not yet, in a relative sense, occurred there, which is not too surprising considering the low educational level (van Klavern 1989, 557).[9]

In a different context, even a political commentator as astute as Hannah Arendt argues that totalitarianism is characterized by the effacement of the public-private distinction (cf. Arendt 1968). Totalitarianism then is a corruption of the separation of the public and private, a pathological negation of the separation of the public from the private, and it is certainly less desirable than the normal articulation of the public/private split in liberal societies. In this respect, Arendt is no more capable of going beyond the essentialist bourgeois conception of the public and private than the mainstream theories of modernization and development are.

---

[8] In addition to most of the contributions in what is undoubtedly the best known and most authoritative collection of readings on the subject, Heidenheimer, Johnston, and LeVine's *Political Corruption: A Handbook* (1989), there are hundreds of essays in this tradition to be found in the many mainstream journals that cater to area studies and comparative politics, particularly in reference to Asia, South America, Africa, and Eastern and Southern Europe.

[9] Most commentators on political corruption, including van Klavern, would readily admit that corruption occurs even in liberal capitalist societies: the main question is whether it exists as a transgression of accepted rules and institutional norms or whether it exists in a systemic way. Similarly, the question is often presented as one of frequency; corruption exists everywhere, but there are pathological elements in underdeveloped societies that result in it being much more common there than in the developed world. "Corruption obviously exists in all societies, but it is also obviously more common in some societies than in others and more common at some times in the evolution of a society than at other times" (Huntington 1989, 377).

Rules of Separation: From Leviticus to Washington, D.C.

The writings and categorizations of academics, however, are not the cause of the division between what is considered a normal and a pathological ordering of the public and private. The academic categories are no more than reflections of the categories and normative precepts prevalent in bourgeois societies themselves. As such, what we must understand is how bourgeois societies come to form and regulate their conception of normalcy regarding the public/private split.

As Canguilhem first argued in *The Normal and the Pathological*, and as Foucault demonstrated in his various histories of the practices of normalization (especially *Madness and Civilization*), the question is not simply one of how the normal is constituted, but how the normal is constituted by way of the production of the pathological. The "normal" in the case of corruption, just as it is in the case of physiological diseases and mental disorders, is largely a negative category; normal is that which is not pathological. And how do we know what is pathological? There are rules that inform us of what is pathological. The term normal itself derives from the Latin term *norma*, rule. The normal is that which conforms to the rule. Conforming to the rule when it comes to political corruption thus refers to *not* transgressing the rules that regulate the purity of the public and private. If breaking these rules is constitutive of the pathological, corruption, then following the rules can be nothing but the normal, good and desirable.[10] If we are to understand how the normal is constituted, we must be able to identify those rules that define the pathological and upon whose presence the fetish of the public depends.

Mary Douglas's analysis of the rules of separation is a useful point of departure for such an analysis. As already noted above, Douglas argues that societies will tend to declare "any object or idea likely to confuse cherished classifications" as impure/dirty/corrupt. These classifications, in turn, are themselves dependant upon a conceptual edifice "whose keystone, boundaries, margins, and internal lines are held in relation by rituals of separation." Most interesting in terms of its implications toward the analytical task at hand is how Douglas applies these principles in her explanation of the various rules regarding clean and unclean food in Leviticus. Douglas attempts to solve what has long been considered a puzzle by biblical scholars, how to explain why some animals are considered unclean and others clean:

> Why should the camel, the hare, and the rock badger be unclean? Why should some locusts, but not all, be unclean? Why should the frog be clean and the mouse and the hippopotamus

---

[10] Recall the definition of corruption by Carl Friedrich cited earlier: "Corruption is a kind of behavior which deviates from the norm actually prevalent or believed to prevail in a given context, such as the political."

unclean? What have chameleons, moles and crocodiles got in
common that they should be listed together (Douglas 1966,
42)?[11]

What makes this a puzzle is that the only information one has regarding these
rules are the rules themselves; there are no other sources from the time of their
creation to explain the logic and reasoning behind them. As Douglas notes, there
have tended to be two ways of addressing this problem. One, that these rules are
arbitrary, irrational, and unexplainable or, two, that they largely serve educational and disciplinary functions—such as the teaching of self-discipline by selecting the most tasty and tempting of creatures as unclean, the selecting of those
animals that were most likely to harm health and carry disease, or the develop-
ing of rules to protect Jewish culture from the encroachment of neighboring cultures (Douglas 1966, 30–33 and 44–50). Having identified the contradictions
and inconsistencies in all of these attempts to explain the rules, Douglas attempts a new explanation by treating these various rules as exactly what they
purport to be: rules of separation. Douglas notes that the traditional idea of the
"holy" was quite literal; it referred to wholeness, completeness, purity of form
(Douglas 1966, 51–53). Thus, for example, animals appropriate for sacrifice had
to be complete and pure, free from physical imperfections and blemishes. Similarly, for "wholeness" and "completeness" to be realized, the organization of the
world has to be kept pure. In accordance with this meaning of holy, we find in-
junctions against sowing the same field with more than one kind of seed, against
plant and animal hybrids, against making cloth by combining two or more kinds
of fibers, against bestiality, and so forth. To be heterodox and confusing is un-
holy; things should be kept in their proper order and not mixed.[12]

Clean and unclean foods then have nothing to do with how appetizing
or ugly or healthy or sloppy the animals are but, rather, how pure they are in
terms of conforming to their classification. The animals true to life in the sky are
birds; they have feathers, two feet, and fly. All those birds that do not fly are
unclean since they defy these principles, as do all those things that fly but are
not birds. The animals true to life in the water are fish with scales and fins; all
those creatures in the water that do not have these characteristics are unclean.
Animals who roam the earth are four-footed and move by walking, jumping, or
hopping. Those animals who seem to have two feet and two hands, like crocodiles, mice, and weasels, are unclean. All that swarms is unclean, since that
mode of propulsion is not proper to either sky, land, or water. Thus, worms,

---

[11] Douglas, mistakenly, assumes that frogs are clean because they are not listed by name
in the relevant sections of Leviticus. She explains this apparent anomaly of a lizard being
clean as a result of frogs having four feet and jumping (as opposed to other lizards, which
do not have four feet and swarm and creep). That frogs, despite their four feet and hopping, are unclean can easily be explained by their amphibious nature.
[12] The common dictum "cleanliness is next to godliness," apparently derived from an old
Hebrew proverb, makes sense in this context.

snakes, and the like are unclean. Some kinds of locusts are clean because they hop; if they fly they have an attribute that only birds can properly have. Proper mammals have cloven feet and chew their cud. Camels, pigs, badgers, and hares all lack one or both of these qualifications, so they are unclean. Members of the antelope family, sheep, goats, cows, and so on do conform to these rules so they are clean (cf. Douglas 1966, 56–58).

This example that Douglas provides us with is important for its illustration of the idea of cleanliness as keeping things in their proper place. Moreover, she provides us with a model for interpreting other sets of rules of separation. The task of interpreting rules of separation when it comes to political corruption seems somewhat different from interpreting Leviticus because we already know what the basic idea behind the rules against political corruption is: to keep private interests from contaminating the public good. So, while Douglas's interpretation of Leviticus is compelling in its elegance and in its ability to explain all the seemingly anomalous classifications of clean/unclean, it would appear that it would not be of much utility for the question of examining rules regarding political corruption. This would be a false conclusion because we only know the general principle behind keeping the public/private divisions separate and clean. Why, for example, is it okay for a congressperson to go on a seven-day trip that is paid for by a lobbyist but not eight days? Why is clientelism corruption and passing laws that benefit campaign supporters and contributors usually not? Why are staff members allowed to lobby the congressional representatives they worked for after one year and not four or five years, or never, or right away? The reality is that, with one naive and potentially, for the state and the capitalist class, disastrous exception that will be examined later on in this chapter, there has never in the history of the modern state been a law against political corruption as such. There are only laws against particular examples of what could be classified as political corruption: bribery, embezzlement, nepotism, and so forth. So, although there is no need to deduce the general principle regarding political corruption, there is a need to examine the rules designed to maintain the purity and separation of the public and private if we are to be able to deduce the ideas behind what bourgeois societies understand to be corruption and what they do not.

In order to make the subsequent discussion easier to follow, a partial list of ethics rules from the House of Representative is to be found in the Appendix. The rules are divided according to the kind of activity they refer to, and the wording of each rule is exactly as it appears in a summary memo of ethics rules that is given to all members, officials, and employees of the House of Representatives (Committee on Standards of Official Conduct 2001). We find all the important components of the concept of corruption that have been already identified and discussed present in these rules. The two bodies principle is present in those rules that distinguish between the person as a public servant and as a private citizen. Gifts from family, other members of Congress, close friends, and anything paid for by public funds are allowed (since in all these exchanges it is either a private-to-private or public-to-public relationship). Hospitality in a private home is allowed as long as that person is not a registered lobbyist (thus negating the distinction of a "private" home). Members must abstain from voting on and lobbying for issues they have private interests in. Similarly, omnipresent in these rules is the general prohibition against mixing the public and private. All of the rules are manifestations of this principle; the suggestion to "avoid mixing of House and private resources" seems clear enough. In this way, the main contours of these rules clearly conform to the dual conceptual principles of two bodies and of corruption as a mixing of categories.

An interesting grey area is the position of the political candidate. When it comes to incumbent members of the House, their reelection campaigns are clearly not on the "public" side of the equation, Congressional staff and resources are not to be used for campaign purposes. No campaign activity, including soliciting contributions, is to take place in any congressional rooms or offices. Even informational mailings to constituents are not allowed ninety days prior to a primary or general election since it would be quite impossible to distinguish between the member sending the mailing as a public servant or as a candidate. Conversely, campaign contributions cannot be used for public or for private purposes. It would seem that candidates for office and campaign contributions are neither public nor private; it is an interesting in-between situation; it is a position that is inherently heterodox and "unclean" by its own nature (perhaps equal to larva that, as swarming creatures, are unclean but, once they transform into walking/hopping insects, become perfectly clean). It may be normal to be a private citizen, it may be normal to be a public servant, to be a candidate is to be neither; and, thus, the conceptual position of the candidate must be kept as separate as possible from the usual registers of public and private so as not to create any confusions.

This interesting in-between case aside, the greatest challenge to interpreting these rules of separation is to be able to explain all those possible forms of corruption against which there are no rules and all those rules that appear to be arbitrary or, at least, could easily be different and still conform to the general principles. Why should the limit for allowable gifts be set at $50 and not higher or lower? If it were $60 or $100 or $10, would it not still fulfill the same function and would not the principles behind the rule remain the same? Similarly, how can we interpret some of the more general and loose rules, such as the prohibition against using one's official position for personal gain?

If anything can be gleaned from Douglas's analysis of Leviticus it is that rules of separation are synonymous with the system of ideas; one constitutes the other. There can be no classification of clean and unclean without the rules of separation and no rules without classifications. In this sense, the reason the gift limit is $50 is so that there is a limit, so that there is a rule of separation. Of course, this is not to say that the dollar amount is random or that it could be any amount and still retain its practical function, but the first part to understanding this rule is to understand why there is a need to place a dollar amount as a limit in the first place. Because of the $50 rule, not simply some general principle of public/private separation, we can now identify what conforms to the rule and what does not; we can now identify the normal and pathological when it comes to accepting gifts. In the same way, the general decrees that public office cannot be used for private gain or that gifts and contributions can never be linked to actions that have been taken or that will be taken are utterly meaningless and have no significance. Why else would a nonrelative/friend give a gift to a member of the House or provide a campaign contribution if not as some form of support for an action that was taken or he/she hopes will be taken? It is precisely because everyone knows this to be true that limits are established and the rules of separation are made specific.[13] We find examples of this principle throughout the rules. We know that everyone is potentially a lobbyist so, in order to establish a clear distinction, the categorization "lobbyist" is made a technical term referring to those who are legally registered as such. We know that any number of actions while in office could result in private gain (indeed, just being in office will result in untold numbers of corporations and law firms being willing to pay significant amounts of money to employ these same individuals once they leave office), so we have a multitude of specific rules that tell us what constitutes private gain and what does not. What political corruption is cannot be known without recourse to these rules of separation.

That the limit to gifts should be $50, that privately sponsored travel has four-day and seven-day limits, that additional earned income is limited to $21,765, all have another foundation as well. The dollar limit to gifts could have been set at $1,000 and the basic principle of there being a specific rule by which to determine what is normal and pathological would be sustained. However, it would be more difficult to justify that a gift of that magnitude would not constitute a corruption of the public interest in the eyes of citizens. Obviously, the more the value of a gift, the less believable it is that the person receiving the "gift" was not influenced by it. It may be quite likely that the gift limit could be $100 or that the additional earned income level could be $40,000 and it would be just as believable and efficient as the existing amounts, but the point is that the specific limits in each rule correspond to some basic parameters regarding how such actions are likely to be perceived. A basic principle that underpins much of the content of these rules is that public servants must not engage in behaviors that are too overt and obvious in their illustration of how the concrete "private" body of the public servant conflicts with the presumed purity and objectivity of their abstract "public" body. If former employees and advisors are to lobby you on behalf of an interest group, they should at least wait a year; it looks better. If you do take a trip paid for by private money, don't let it go beyond four days; it doesn't look good. Maybe it is true that elected public servants will tend to act on behalf of important supporters and campaign contributors, but at least don't make it too obvious.

---

[13] Obviously, this general prohibition against linking gifts to past or future actions simply requires that the exchange not be explicitly linked to actions; giving a gift or contribution is fine as long as it is not presented as an exchange for some action.

The investigation into the violation of many of the rules listed above by Representative "Bud" Shuster illustrates this principle. Shuster, chairman of the Transportation and Infrastructure Committee, became the object of an official investigation by the Committee on Standards of Official Conduct (CSOC) largely as a result of the apparent collusion between himself and his former chief of staff, who had worked for him for twenty-two years, lobbyist Ann Eppard (cf. CSOC 2000a). Eppard, after resigning her post, established her own lobbying firm and lobbied Shuster on behalf of her clients during and after the twelve-month period following her resignation. As already noted, senior house staff are not allowed to lobby their former employers for twelve months following the end of their employment. The official report notes that this restriction, enacted in 1989, was intended *"to diminish any appearance that Government decisions might be affected by the improper use by an individual of his former senior position "* (italics in original, CSOC 2000a, 8).

Shuster and Eppard proved to be pretty inept at keeping up appearances. Not only was Eppard the former chief of staff, she was also, while she was lobbying Shuster, the assistant treasurer for Shuster's reelection campaign and a significant fund-raiser (in itself, it is perfectly legal to be a lobbyist and a campaign officer or fund-raiser—it simply must not *appear* to be something that is done in exchange for some favor). Shortly after Eppard began to represent Frito-Lay and Federal Express, Shuster pushed through Congress the granting of a waiver from many federal safety regulations for midsized delivery trucks (such as those used by both companies); "a quiet lobbying campaign aimed at the House Transportation Committee yielded in a few months what years of regulatory struggles had not" (CSOC 2000a, 79). After Eppard was hired by Amtrak, Shuster championed a bill that provided Amtrak with money and financial restructuring, exactly what Amtrak had hired Eppard to accomplish. After Eppard was hired by the Outdoor Advertising Association of America, Shuster argued on behalf of and legislation was eventually passed that allows more billboards to be placed along routes designated as scenic byways (cf. CSOC 2000a, 79–82). There are a great many additional potential rules infractions investigated by the CSOC including a trip by Shuster to Puerto Rico paid for by one of Eppard's clients and frequent stays by Shuster at Eppard's home and his frequent use of her car.

It should be noted that the CSOC found Shuster to not be guilty of any infractions when it came to the three legislative cases noted above. Although he was found to have violated the letter of the law when it came to the twelve-month rule and gift rules as well as being guilty of some bad campaign finance accounting and a few other minor infractions, all the infractions boil down to the violation of one rule, literally rule 1, clause I of the Code of Official Conduct: "a Member, officer, or employee of the House of Representatives shall conduct himself at all times in a manner which shall reflect creditably on the House of Representatives." What Shuster was ultimately found guilty of is not being a good enough actor when it comes to maintaining the fetish of the public. The Letter of Reproval issued to Shuster by the CSOC reads like a mantra to clause

I; it begins by noting "by your actions you have brought discredit to the House of Representatives" and goes on to establish why each infraction constitutes a violation of clause I:

> The first area of misconduct, constituting conduct that did not reflect creditably on the House of Representatives. . . . The third area of misconduct to which you admitted, and which constitutes conduct by you that did not reflect creditably on the House of Representatives . . . The fifth area of misconduct to which you have admitted, and which constitutes conduct that did not reflect creditably on the House of Representatives. (CSOC 2000b)

The letter concludes with the following statement:

> In our free and democratic system of republican government, it is vital that citizens feel confidence in the integrity of the legislative institutions that make the laws that govern America. Ultimately, individual Members of Congress can undermine respect for the institutions of our government. (CSOC 2000b)

The purity of the public is specular and illusionary, a performative gesture, a product of a series of rules designed to cloak the fetishistic nature of the public/private split. In Leviticus, the division between the clean and unclean was such that by following the rules of separation one could completely realize the conceptual goal of wholeness as it was understood at the time. In Washington, D.C., the fetishistic nature of the public makes it impossible to fully realize the separation of the public and private in terms of the actual content of politics. The legal fiction, as Kantorowicz terms it, of the abstract body of the public is materialized and regulated through the rules of separation, in that what is kept pure is not politics itself but, rather, its categorizations and self-presentations. Given the impossibility of removing "private interests" from either the real bodies of public servants or from the actual substance of bourgeois politics, a series of rules and practices is instituted in order to purge the realm of appearances from acts that challenge the categorization of society as divided into two mutually exclusive registers, the public and private. The success of these rules of separation thus relies upon two interrelated principles: to regulate and cloak or eliminate all those activities that are likely to be perceived by citizens as a presence of private regarding within the public body, and to structure the parameters and boundaries of what citizens are likely to perceive as corruption, since the rules serve as the point of reference for establishing what constitutes the normal and pathological in such matters.

That the rules discussed above do not include a great many potential corruptions of the public by the private can only be interpreted as a sign that they fall within the "normal" side of the equation. It could easily be argued that members of the Congress are corrupt when they vote according to the private interests of constituents in their districts, or that a president is corrupt when he appoints his friends to public office, and so forth. We find nothing against these types of activities in the existing rules of separation, although in both cases it could be a violation of the rules if appearances are not maintained.[14] The pragmatic requisites of bourgeois politics necessitate that private interests be everywhere within the "public" but that everyone categorize these short circuits as being normal and desirable.

In this respect, the rules of separation found in Leviticus and those found in Washington, D.C. are not based on some really existing truth in nature or society but are attempts to formalize and ritualize the meanings and categorizations through which society maps its understandings and perceptions. The attempt to explain the rules of separation by reference to the "real" dirtiness imminent in the object or activity itself is thus necessarily bound to failure. Pigs and shrimp are no more "dirty," from the perspective of nature and biology, than are cows and tuna. Clientelism is no more "dirty," from the perspective of the nature of the interests it articulates, than are pluralist interest group arrangements. Again, to go back to Douglas, it is only in reference to the system of ideas that these rules make sense, and their object is nothing more than the material constitution and reproduction of the system of ideas.

The Australian Case: Fetishism Revealed

That political corruption as such has never been completely outlawed in modern societies thus makes perfect sense, because the whole point of the discourse and practices surrounding corruption has been to make most cases of private regarding within the public acceptable and normal by identifying only the some forms of private regarding as "corrupt." If ever there was to be a general rule that no private interests are allowed in the public arena, politics as we know it would be impossible and every public servant would potentially be guilty of some version of corruption. A fascinating exception to this general principle of rules of separation necessarily being specific and partial so as to legitimize all those typical

---

[14] Such as with the savings and loan scandals of the late 1980s, it is almost always acceptable for members of Congress to lend support to business interests, but when it appears as being "too much" support, whatever that may be judged to be, it can be said to violate the rules of separation precisely because people judge it as "too much," because it does not "reflect creditably" on the state apparatuses. When it comes to having supported savings and loans that failed and cost taxpayers billions of dollars, it appears the threshold for what constitutes "too much" is lower than usual. In this respect, it may very well be the case that the only reason Shuster was investigated and reproved by the CSOC is because the *Journal of Commerce* published an article raising suspicions about Shuster's activities and because he was also the object of an investigation by the *60 Minutes* television program.

forms of private regarding is the Australian attempt to eliminate political corruption. The Australians have come the closest of all to outlawing political corruption in its most general sense, and their misadventures allow us to see how the conceptual edifice of the bourgeois state may unravel when it is faced with a literal prohibition of private regarding within its institutions.

In the wake of a series of corruption scandals in the 1980s, various Australian states adopted legislation designed to combat political corruption. In 1989, corruption commissions were established in three Australian states: the Independent Commission against Corruption (ICAC) in New South Wales, the Official Corruption Commission (OCC) in Western Australia, and the Criminal Justice Commission (CJC) in Queensland. What is fascinating in these cases is not only the degree to which particular types of political corruption are made illegal but also how these commissions attempted to outlaw political corruption as such.

We find in the ICAC Act a general prohibition on "corrupt conduct" in unusually broad terms and in ways that come very close to the general understanding of corruption as any mixing of the public and private. For the ICAC, corrupt conduct is:

> (a) any conduct of any person (whether or not a public official) that adversely affects, or that could adversely affect, either directly or indirectly, the honest or impartial exercise of official functions by any public official, any group of public officials; or
>
> (b) any conduct of a public official that constitutes or involves the dishonest or partial exercise of any of his or her official functions; or
>
> (c) any conduct of a public official or former public official that constitutes or involves a breach of public trust; or
>
> (d) any conduct of a public official or former public official that involves the misuse of information or material that he or she has acquired in the course of his or her official functions, whether or not for his or her benefit or for the benefit of any other person. (Committee on Government [COG] 1995, 237–238)

Rather than use the term "corrupt conduct," the CJC uses the term "official misconduct" but defines it almost exactly the same way:

> (a) conduct of a person, whether or not the person holds an appointment in a unit of public administration, that adversely affects, or could adversely affect, directly or indirectly, the

honest and impartial discharge of functions or exercise of powers or authority of a unit of public administration or any person holding an appointment in a unit of public administration; or

(b) conduct of a person while the person holds or held an appointment in a unit of public administration—

(i) that constitutes or involves the discharge of the person's functions of exercise of his or her authority, as the holder of the appointment, in a manner that is not honest or is not impartial; or

(ii) that constitutes or involves a breach of the trust placed in the person by reason of his or her holding the appointment in a unit of public administration; or

(c) conduct that involves the misuse by any person of information or material that the person has acquired in or in connection with the discharge of his or her functions or exercise of his or her powers or authority as the holder of an appointment in a unit of public administration, whether the misuse is for the benefit of the person or another person. (COG 1995, 241–242)

The OCC rules are also very similar and include the distinction between "corrupt conduct" (in effect, all conduct by public officials that violates the criminal code) and "improper conduct" (conduct that is defined exactly the way the ICAC defines "corrupt conduct" and the CJC defines "official misconduct") (COG 1995, 45–46).

Whether it is termed "corrupt conduct," "official misconduct," or "improper conduct," the Australians have attempted to outlaw any breach of objectivity, any impure action/nonaction by all public servants. When compared with the ethics rules found in the U.S. Congress, the Australian rules seem extremely general and ambitious. There are an almost unlimited number of potential infractions that could constitute "corrupt conduct." Not only is it enough to show some lack of objectivity, but also the possibility that some conduct could result in such a lack, directly or indirectly, could result in that conduct being considered corrupt. It would be possible, for example, to argue that some elected officials were not objective because they were making decisions and engaging in conduct that was focused upon their reelection possibilities and not the objective and full exercise of their official functions, or that bureaucrats were corrupt for putting the interests of their institutions and offices above the public good, or that members of the parliament were voting according to party lines and, thus, were corrupt because they were putting the cohesion and interests of the party above the need for members of parliament to be objective. Any nonpublic regarding could constitute corrupt conduct. Of course, just because there are many kinds of conduct that could be considered corrupt given the above definitions does not mean that the various corruption commissions have applied and interpreted these new rules in particularly broad ways. Although the political institutions of Australia have not self-destructed and we do not find thousands of public servants seeking asylum from corruption commissions gone amuck, there are some illuminating examples of how the expansive nature of these rules has come into conflict with what most would consider "normal" conduct by public servants.

The ICAC case involving Terry Metherell is probably the most clear and famous example of conduct typical of public servants being found corrupt.[15] In April 1992, Metherell, a member of the parliament in New South Wales, resigned from his position and accepted an appointment as a director of the Environmental Protection Agency. Metherell, a former member of the Liberal Party, was one of five independent members of the parliament that was otherwise split with forty-seven members belonging to the Liberal Party and forty-seven members belonging to the Australian Labor Party; Nick Greiner, of the Liberal Party, was the premier for New South Wales (ICAC 1992a, 6–8).[16] Metherell's resignation allowed the Liberal Party to regain his seat and take a one-seat lead over the Australian Labor Party. That the Liberal Party benefited from Metherell's resignation and that they had appointed him to a well-paying position the same day he resigned were the reasons that the case was investigated as a potential case of political corruption.

The ICAC found Nick Greiner (and one other minister, Tim Moore) guilty of having engaged in corrupt conduct. The reasoning behind the finding was that "the conduct of each man involved partial exercise of his official functions, that it involved a breach of the public trust, and that it could involve reasonable grounds for their dismissal as Ministers" (ICAC 1992b, 4).[17] The appointment of Metherell was obviously not based on who could best serve the public good but rather on the political gains that could be realized by Metherell resigning from his elected office. Greiner acted in terms of what was in the best interest of the Liberal Party (and, thus, also himself) and, by so doing, was obviously not acting in an objective way and in a way that conformed to the full exercise of his official functions (recall the ICAC definition of corrupt conduct noted earlier). Greiner attacked the logic of the ICAC definition of corrupt conduct in his testimony, declaring that it constituted the end of politics:

---

[15] The significance of the Metherell case to the question of corruption has been discussed by Philp (1997). Philp cites the case to illustrate the difficulties of defining political corruption in a satisfactory way.

[16] Metherell had been a member of the Liberal Party; he had even been the Minister of Education and Youth Affairs in the Greiner administration of 1988–1991; he left the party in October 1991 (ICAC 1992a, 6).

[17] Greiner and Moore resigned their Ministerial positions and left parliament following the ICAC findings. The ICAC decisions were later declared null by the Court of Appeals.

If what the Minister for the Environment did and what I did was corrupt, then in my judgment every political appointment that has ever been made in this State was corrupt. It will not be the case of the Leader of the Opposition or of a Leader in the Upper House reserving for themselves certain positions that they intend to use for political appointments. It will simply be against the law . . . Ultimately, if what we have done was against the law, then all honorable members need to understand that it is, for practical purposes, the death of politics in this State. Once a political party is elected to office it will be against the law for it to make decisions which are in any way influenced by political considerations . . . Under the English common law very serious obligations to act in the public interest are placed on those elected to public office, and yet our highest public officials are at the same time part of a political system which is about what is in many ways a largely private interest in terms of winning or holding a seat or holding office. This is a very difficult philosophical matter. In simple terms, the philosophy, which was once called disinterestedness, meant that once elected to Parliament members were obliged to ignore the interests of their constituents and act only in what they considered to be the national interest. We here in Australia chose not to adopt that view of parliamentary office . . . But every member needs to understand that the standards that are implied in this censure of me today are entirely new standards and are very strict standards. I am not sure, when honorable members have considered them calmly in the bright light of day, that those standards are going to produce a workable system of democracy in our State. (ICAC 1992a, 65)

Ironically, it was Greiner and the Liberal Party that had established the ICAC in 1989.

This remarkable testimony by Greiner gets to the heart of the matter. If his actions are corrupt, then all of modern politics is corrupt; private interests are inherent to politics as we know it. By making political corruption as such illegal, the ICAC has declared politics illegal.[18] The House ethics rules discussed

---

[18] The ICAC was troubled enough by this case and Greiner's testimony that it took the time to reconsider its definitions of corrupt conduct. In considering the arguments for and against any changes to the existing laws, the ICAC did not suggest any changes. It reiterated the logic of why the definition was so broad as to include conduct that could be seen as inherent to the system and argued that the partial and unobjective exercise of public office can be just as damaging to the public good whether it is the product of bribery or the product of more systemic institutional and cultural forces (cf. ICAC 1992b, 14–15).

earlier have the effect of declaring a great multiplicity of presences of the private within the public normal and acceptable by establishing rules of separation that declare only some forms of this presence as pathological. The United States, and every other modern state, knows that a true and substantive lack of the private within the public is impossible in bourgeois society. As already noted, the functional role of the rules of separation is not to regulate the actual substance of politics but, rather, to keep the categories we use to perceive, describe, and comprehend modern politics clean, pure, intact, and believable. What the ICAC rules accomplish, as the Metherell case illustrates, is exactly the opposite. By taking the idea of political corruption literally and seriously, the ICAC is making visible to everyone that the abstract body of the public is nothing more than a fetish, nothing more than private interests acting "as if" they were the national interest and that public servants are always and necessarily concrete individuals who are required, by the requisites of maintaining the social existence of the state, to act "as if" they also possessed an abstract body.

I do not mean to suggest that the ICAC with its definition of corrupt conduct has single-handedly destroyed the conceptual edifice of the Australian state or the fiction inherent in the private/public split, although it certainly does not help them. What the ICAC does is to enable us to appreciate the importance of rules of separation in the constitution of the public/private split in contemporary societies. The division of society into two bodies, the public and the private, so integral and constitutive of the state itself, relies upon rules and rituals/everyday practices that constantly reaffirm and reassert the naturalness and compulsion of this division. The exchange of commodities provides the everyday foundation for the existence of the categories intrinsic to the two bodies doctrine and its embodiments in contemporary bourgeois societies. Rules and rituals of separation help institute and reproduce these embodiments by maintaining the purity of the categories in the face of the constant threat that the fetishistic status of the public body will become so obvious that individuals will no longer accept the integrity of the categorizations that constitute it.

4

The National Individual and the Machine of Enjoyment; or, The Dangers of Baseball, Hot Dogs, and Apple Pie

> The denial of the instituting dimension of society, the covering up of the instituting imaginary by the instituted imaginary, goes hand in hand with the creation of true-to-form individuals, whose thought and life are dominated by repetition (whatever else they may do, they do very little), whose radical imagination is bridled to the utmost degree possible, and who are hardly truly individualized.
> —Cornelius Castoriadis, *Philosophy, Politics, Autonomy*

Having covered the production of the public/private distinction, our efforts must now turn to the production of the political community as a national and territorially bounded entity. As noted in the discussion of the Greek *polis*, a distinguishing feature of the state is its spatial organization in national-territorial terms.[1] Part of the logic behind the necessity of territoriality was already identified in the discussion of Elias and his concept of the monopoly mechanism; the proper functioning of a state presupposes a cohesive and unified population qua political community. More on the functionality of the national political community toward the state follows. The main theoretical and conceptual problem, however, is not to understand this process from the functionalist point of view of the state and its needs (as the literature review below shows, this is fairly easy and has been done by many a political theorist). The main problem is to understand

---

[1] It should be noted that a political community defined in terms of nationality also conforms to the abstract/concrete dichotomy discussed earlier. This is so because the nation is never reducible to any concrete group of individuals but, rather, is presumably both beyond all its individual manifestations and transhistorical. Thus, the relationship between the public/private division and the national political community is one where the abstract nature of the community allows for the fiction of a "national" or "public" interest even in the absence of any shared interests between the actual individuals who happen to find themselves within this community.

how such a great multitude of people come to think of themselves as members of a nation and actually relish and treasure this identification. The problem is to understand how the national community is actually produced through the materiality of the everyday.

The study of national identity has always been a key moment within political and social theory. One axis of theorizing has revolved around the questions of essentialism and historiography and ranges from German idealism to contemporary Marxist and poststructuralist theory. Within this grouping, whose figures include Schiller, Fichte, and Herder on one side and Anderson (1991) and Hobsbawn (1990) on the other, the key question involves the naturalness and goodness of national identity or, the opposite, its contingent and constructed character. This very wide and central theoretical couplet is one that I will largely avoid in this chapter. I take it as a given that national identity is "imagined" and it is a product of multiple cultural and political projects and processes. Although sympathetic to many of the arguments in Anderson and Hobsbawn as well as their attempts to counter nationalist historiography and its allied literatures, this chapter engages in a very different debate and is in dialogue with a different set of theories. The discussion here is directed toward the mechanisms through which society forges national identifications and not toward the more elusive and polemical task of countering the nationalist ordering of history and narrative.[2]

From Rousseau to Easton, Identifying the Problem

> A people, says Grotius, can give itself to a king. According to Grotius, therefore, a people is a people before it gives itself to a king. This gift itself is a civil act; it presupposes a public deliberation. Thus, before examining the act whereby a people chooses a king, it would be well to examine the act whereby a people is a people. For since this act is necessary prior to the other, it is the true foundation of society.
> —Jean-Jacques Rousseau, *On the Social Contract*

At least since Rousseau's *Social Contract*, political theory has recognized that the constitution of a "people" or "political community" is a necessary condition for the existence of the state. In what amounts to an epistemic break with the social contract tradition, Rousseau notes the logical necessity of the constitution

---

[2] A concurrent problem is the emphasis on "narration" and rhetoric. This is an elitist emphasis—the lives and temporal rhythms of the masses are ignored. The ideas and utterances of novelists, politicians, and other intellectuals are raised to the level of historical agents. Such arguments conform very well to the idea that history is the product of great men and their deeds. Furthermore, often the tendency in this literature has been to look backwards, to try to give some indication of how nations were produced rather than examine the mechanisms that constantly *reproduce* the national community.

of a people prior to the constitution of the state.[3] Accordingly, Rousseau concludes that the first social contract must be an internal one between the individual as citizen and the individual as agent within the state of nature (cf. Althusser 1982, 113–160). The outcome of this "contract" is the emergence of a "people" or "political community" qua sovereign.[4]

Although not necessarily recognizing or stressing the ontological argument put forth by Rousseau, contemporary political theory has recognized the importance and functionality of a cohesive political community for the existence and legitimation of state power. Seymour Martin Lipset takes it as axiomatic that "all states that have recently gained independence are faced with two interrelated problems, legitimating the use of political power and establishing national identity" (1963, 21). In David Easton's model of the political system, national identities are supports of the first order. More important than support of regime or government is support for the political community, since a political system is not only unlikely to function but *even to exist* without this requisite support (cf. Easton 1965, 171–219). For Easton, the concept of a political community conveys the necessity of "some cohesive cement—a sense or feeling of community among its members" (1965, 176). Easton's use of the term "political community" is not merely synonymous with the nation-state, it is inclusive of it and constitutes the most modern version of community (leaving aside supranational organizations).

Easton's examination of the conditions that contribute to or cause the formation of this "cohesive cement" illustrates the analytical weakness of approaches that have arisen from what John Gunnell (1993) has termed the "behavioral reformation" within political theory. Easton identifies politicization as the general cause of this identification with political community:

> Concrete responses for the expression and reinforcement of a sense of community appear in patriotic ceremonies, the physical symbols of group identity such as totems, flags, songs, canonized heroes and, in literate societies, even in such trivial manifestations as the coloring of territorial maps . . . But since responses such as these are so well known, they present no special problems for purposes of macroanalysis and we need probe no further in this direction. (Easton 1965, 332)

For Easton, the role of politicization in engendering support of community is fairly simple and unproblematic. Behaviors are rewarded and punished in order to socialize the individual in a way consistent with the given political commu-

---

[3] The assertion that a people must exist "before" the state need not refer to a temporal distinction of one existing before the other in historical time. It does, however, necessarily refer to the logical position of one vis-à-vis the other.

[4] As Althusser notes, it is not a true contract since one of its parties, the community or people, comes to exist only after the contract is made (Althusser 1982, 123–134).

nity. Easton, however, recognized that the kind of identification needed for political communities was stronger than that which typical behaviorist arguments about socialization/politicization could explain. After all, identifications that may lead a citizen to risk his life in war and that effectively displace competing identifications (tribe, region, race, class, or religion) presuppose something more than mere socialization (which is the behaviorist explanation for these other identifications as well). For this reason, Easton stresses that although politicization is the general cause of community identification, ideology represents a "special" cause. Easton argued that the "we-feeling" necessary for the community to exist, stems from a shared history and experience that lead people to think of themselves as a political entity of common origin and destiny. This experience and, especially, history must be made intelligible in a way that their effect is precisely this we-feeling:

> Whether we are referring to the shared history of the members of a system or to the current collective experiences, if these factors are to have any impact on the community feelings of the members of the system and especially upon upcoming generations, they must be interpreted and codified in a form that makes them readily visible, accessible, and transmissible over the generations. Ideology performs this function for the political community. (Easton 1965, 333)

Karl Deutsch makes a similar argument (Deutsch 1953, 60–80). While Easton stresses the necessity of a common system of meanings and interpretations qua ideology, Deutsch argues that a "people" is the product of complimentary communicative habits that allow for efficient communication among those who constitute a "people." This efficiency of communication provides the basis for the cohesion of a people, and it explains why those who do not share these communicative habits would be viewed as external to a given nationality or peoplehood.

These behaviorist accounts of national identity fail to effectively explain the source of this identification. In Easton's case, a descriptive account of ideology is offered without any causal understanding of how such an ideology may come about or why anyone would accept or internalize this ideology. As in the case of politicization, ideology remains an "independent variable," something that explains rather than something to be explained. With Deutsch, the argument is circular; that which causes identification with the nation, the efficiency of communication, is concurrently presented as the definition of nationality. By definition, Deutsch's argument always holds true, and thus explains nothing, since wherever we find such "efficient" communication we find national identification and vice versa. Deutsch in effect argues that culture determines culture or nationality determines nationality.[5]

> Taken all together, they [habits of communication] include, therefore, in particular the elements of that which anthropologists call culture. If these elements are in fact sufficiently complementary, they will add up to an integrated pattern or configuration of communicating, remembering, and acting, that is, to a culture in the sense of the citations quoted earlier in our discussion; and the individuals who have these complementary habits, vocabularies, and facilities are what we call a people. (Deutsch 1953, 71)

Behaviorist political theory's weaknesses are shared by more recent and radical attempts to explain national identities. Immanuel Wallerstein explains national identities (along with racial and ethnic identities) as a function of the division of labor within and between states (Balibar and Wallerstein 1991, 71–85). Wallerstein argues that national identities arise from the political structuring of the modern world system into states and the functionality of national

---

[5] Nonetheless, Deutsch's arguments are quantifiable, which seems to be his main theoretical goal. In his review of previous theories of nationalism he states that "in all the works surveyed, these findings were qualitative rather than quantitative. Not merely had measurements not been made, but the very concepts themselves furnished no bases for them. Where predictions were nonetheless attempted, their reliability was small on the average, and sporadic at best" (Deutsch 1953, 14). In the many years since the publication of Deutsch's book, we have seen the truth regarding the ability and precision of quantitative social science to predict the rise and fall of nationalism.

A Hegelian reading of Deutsch on this issue, however, transforms what may be a circular definition into an ontological statement about the substance of nationalism. If we restate Deutsch's definition as "the nation is the nation" we return to the formula for Universality and self-identity found in Hegel's *Science of Logic*. By defining nationality only in relation to itself, Deutsch in effect empties the category nation of all particularities by not reducing it to any determinations (Nation is family, Nation is ideology, etc.); nation is its own negation in this definition, and the identity nation becomes Universal form emptied of all content and particulars. This definition represents the unity of Nation beyond its particular properties. As Žižek has noted, this Universal form, emptied of all content and representing ideal unity, constitutes the qualitative One that is necessary for any quantitative discussion. "A reference to the 'logic of the signifier' may help here: the One is what Lacan calls 'pure signifier', the signifier 'without signified', the signifier which does not designate any positive properties of the object since it refers only to its pure notional Unity brought about performatively by this signifier itself (the exemplary case of it is, of course, proper names)—and the Void: is it not precisely *the signified of this pure signifier?* This Void, the signified of the One, is the *subject* of the signifier: the One represents the Void (the subject) for the other signifiers—which others? Only on the basis of the One of quality can one arrive at the One of quantity; at the One as the first in a series of counting" (Žižek 1991, 52).

identities to the internal cohesion of a given state as well as their usefulness for engendering mass support in the interstate battles for hierarchy within the global division of labor (thus insuring the state against internal and external threats). Wallerstein seeks to explain national identity simply from its functionality toward the state. Again, this approach fails to explain why anyone would take on these identities and the conditions necessary for such identification to take place.

This common shortcoming stems from the false dichotomy of the individual and the collective posited by the theories discussed above. Although Easton, Deutsch, and Wallerstein rely on an unsatisfactory use of functional causality (the functionality of national identification toward the state explains its existence), an even deeper problem is their assumption of already existing individuals who, through their national identities, combine into a collective whole.[6] Put another way, the problem of national identities is the problem of the subject. This was already present in Rousseau since the agency of the state could only come out of the already existing agency of the people. The people, in turn, could not be presupposed but had to be a product of an already existing and real process. For the "people" or "nation" to possess positive ontological status, it must be constituted by something "real," something that can be said to have being. If we assume that the individual de facto possesses positive ontological status, the problem is simply to understand the combining of individuals into a people. But if we consider the individual to be socially determined, the individual only gains existence through the collective or society. The assumption that the individual "exists" outside and as the foundation of society is inverted. For this reason, the behaviorist question of why individuals combine as a community can never be fully answered in its own terms. In searching for the causes of the combining of individuals into a collective, the question of why an individual would act or behave in this way necessarily must make reference to some "belief," "preference," or "motive" that underpins such action. The behaviorist answer to this question is contradictory and circular because concurrent with the presumption of the autonomous individual is the assumption that his social behavior shapes his beliefs. This results in explanations, such as Easton's, which at times argue that the individual is autonomous (the demands placed upon the system are a product of rational action, behavior is a product of belief and free will) but at other times argue that the beliefs of the individual are a product of behavior (as in the politicization of individuals as members of the community). Behaviorism's assumptions preclude it from arguing that the individual "freely" chooses to become part of the collective just as they preclude it from arguing that the collective preexists the individual and serves as the cause of the individual.

Norbert Elias, once again, has done much to shed light on this conceptual impasse in social and political theory. In *The History of Manners*, Elias attacked the likes of Weber and Parsons for the same problems identified here in the work of Easton and Deutsch and argued that this problem of the individual-

---

[6] For an examination of functional causality, see Elster (1983).

society split is itself a product of the nation-state and its hold over our theoretical thinking:

> The splitting of the image of humanity into an image of man as individual and an image of men as societies has widely ramifying roots. One branch is a very characteristic split in the values and ideals encountered, on close inspection, in all the more developed nation-states, and perhaps most pronounced in nations with a strong liberal tradition. In the development of the value systems of all such nation-states, one finds, on the one hand, a strand which sees society as a whole, the nation, as the highest value; and, on the other, a strand which posits the wholly self-sufficient, free individual, the "closed personality," as the highest value. It is not always easy to harmonize these two "highest values" with one another. But usually this problem is not squarely faced. People talk with great warmth of the freedom and independence of the individual, and with equal warmth of the freedom and independence of their own nation . . . This split in ideals, this contradiction in the ethos by which people are brought up, finds expression in the theories of sociology. (Elias 1978, 245–246)

Elias's suggestion for overcoming this tension in assumptions is to conceive of the individual not as an already existing entity but rather as a process; not as a question of "insides" and "outsides" but rather as the product of social activity itself, which, for him, is neither "inside" nor "outside" the individual since the individual is both constituted by and constituting of this process of individuation (cf. Elias 1978, 245–263).

This conceptual weakness is particularly surprising in the case of Wallerstein, since it is his collaborator, Balibar, who notes that:

> *All identity is individual,* but there is no individual identity that is not historical or, in other words, constructed within a field of social values, norms of behavior and collective symbols. Individuals never identify with one another (not even in the "fusional" practices of mass movements or the "intimacy" of affective relations), nor, however, do they ever acquire an isolated identity, which is an intrinsically contradictory notion. (Balibar and Wallerstein 1991, 94)

The conclusion that all identity is individual thus leads to the question of the constitution of the national individual (not the combining of already existing individuals). Very much in keeping with Elias's critique and suggestions, identification becomes synonymous with individualization, and a theory that explains

national identities must therefore explain the individual rather than take it as an
assumption.

Practice, Ideology, and Interpellation

Balibar derives his assertion that all identity is individual from Althusser's definition of ideology as a "representation of the imaginary relationship of individuals to their real conditions of existence" (Althusser 1971, 162). What distinguishes this definition from Marx's well-known definition of ideology in *The
German Ideology* is the place Althusser assigns to the individual. For Althusser,
ideology only exists by and for the individual. It is through the practices of concrete individuals that ideology comes about. Ideology is lived experience, experience being a product of the sensory perceptions of an individual. Ideology is
no longer a false representation of the real world brought about by the world's
alienating effects. Identities are always individual since they are an effect of
ideology, occurring when the individual is interpellated by "recognizing" itself
as the subject who some utterance or call is directed at (cf. Althusser 1971, 170–
177). This act of "recognition" signifies the point where we experience ourselves or are conscious of ourselves as subjects of a particular identity: "this
recognition only gives us the "consciousness" of our incessant (eternal) practice
of ideological recognition" (Althusser 1971, 173).[7]

This shift from more traditional Marxist views of ideology signifies
the emergence of a theory that has as a goal the explanation of the individual
subject. The explanation of the "I" or "ego" is central to any attempt to explain
the "community" or "people" as a process of individualization. The national
individual, as an object of analysis, is only thinkable by way of Althusser and
psychoanalysis, since no other theoretical traditions allow for this question (with
the notable exception of Spinoza). A significant problem remains, however, for
Althusser never fully reconciled his assertion that ideology is material (practice)
with his assertion that it is ideology that constitutes individuals as subjects by
way of interpellation. After spending most of the first part of his essay examining the materiality of ideology, Althusser conceptualizes interpellation as the
ideological mechanism that explains identity and individualization. Althusser,
however, never explained how ideology produced particular interpellations.
What about the materiality of ideology explains why we do or do not "recognize" ourselves as a given identity? Under what ideological conditions would
someone "recognize" himself as "American" or "worker" or "sinner"?

---

[7] As Spinoza put it, "Experience teaches us no less clearly than reason, that men believe
themselves to be free, simply because they are conscious of their actions, and uncon-
scious of the causes whereby those actions are determined: and, further, it is plain that the
dictates of the mind are but another name for the appetites, and therefore, vary according
to the varying state of the body" (Spinoza 1955, 135).

This deficiency has largely remained unexamined.[8] Most commentators either pay lip service to Althusser's assertion that ideology is material without reference to interpellation or discuss interpellation without reference to ideological practices, reducing it to a discursive idealism where simply language or discourse does the interpellating. In Ernesto Laclau's (1977) famous use of interpellation to examine populism, he lays the agency of the interpellation solely with discourse. For Laclau, the interpellation of individuals as "the people" is a product of the political discourse of the power bloc (those classes and class factions, unified by the state, that hold political power). In nonpopulist moments, the "people" interpellation represents the neutralization of antagonisms between the class factions of the power bloc and the class factions of the people bloc by presenting what may have been understood as antagonism as being simply difference. This becomes populist when it is subverted by some faction of the power bloc in its attempt to become hegemonic (over competing factions of the power bloc) by appealing to the "people" and interpellating them in opposition to the dominant ideology and the state (what was once simply difference becomes antagonism). By recasting difference as antagonism, a faction of the power bloc, in their attempt to redefine the power bloc and assert their hegemony, is able to enlist the "people" as allies against competing power bloc factions (cf. Laclau 1977, 143–198). Laclau makes no reference to the materiality of ideology, and interpellation becomes an idealist category with no reference to the material conditions and constraints that may explain why a particular interpellation works (or fails) or why a particular populist project may have succeeded (or failed).

Göran Therborn's treatise (1980) on ideology and power ignores interpellation altogether. He effectively negates the radical potential of Althusser's assertion that ideology is material by arguing that ideology is discursive while materiality is nondiscursive:

> All human activity is invested with meaning and all ideological interpellations have some kind of "material" existence, in bodily movements, sounds, paper and ink, and so on. This does not mean, however, that it is impossible to distinguish, analytically, ideological from material, discursive from non-

---

[8] Key exceptions to this not only include the work of Žižek, discussed later in this chapter, but also that of Mladen Dolar (1993) and Judith Butler (1997). For Butler, who builds on Dolar's arguments, Althusser's concept of interpellation doesn't work in all cases, love being a prime example. Butler argues that interpellation best fits situations of religious authority and punitive law, where guilt functions as the foundation for interpellation. Thus, Butler argues, we see that Althusser's examples, from the police hailing someone on the street to the kneeling in prayer, are all from this domain. The arguments in this chapter take a different track and do not assume that guilt or other similar motivations function as that which explains why someone (mis)recognizes himself or subjugates himself.

discursive dimensions of human practices. (Therborn 1980,
33)

Having made the "analytical" distinction between ideology and materiality,
Therborn proceeds to treat their relations as external. Ideology exists in the
mind, and its affirmations and sanctions in the "material" matrix either support
or subvert a particular ideology.[9] Thus, ideology is not material, but rather must
conform enough to the existing material matrix so as to make it compelling (cf.
Therborn 1980, 31–49).

Michel Pêcheux (1982) recognized quite well that Althusser's explanation of interpellation was in need of further development. However, there is
no reference to any practice other than discursive in Pêcheux's fleshing out of
the conditions necessary for an interpellation to occur. For Pêcheux, language
assumes the subject since the "I" is always present in discourse. Pêcheux names
this phenomenon the "subject-form of language." This common feature of all
discursive formations is crucial in explaining interpellations since, for Pêcheux
as for Lacan, it is within the network of meanings and utterances that the subject
is constituted: *"the subject is 'caught' in this network*—'common nouns' and
'proper names,' 'shifting' effects, syntactic constructions, etc.—*such that he
results as 'cause of himself'"* (Pêcheux 1982, 108). Pêcheux specifies and re-
fines the mechanism of interpellation as it relates to language, and he outlines
the characteristics language must necessarily possess in order for any interpellation to take place. However, he cannot explain why *particular* interpellations
happen. By limiting his discussion to the discursive elements of interpellation
(i.e., why we are so quick to recognize ourselves as subjects and take it to be
given that indeed we are subjects), he fails to examine the historical and material
practices that could explain why we recognize ourselves as any particular identity.

Although each of the references above failed to overcome a weakness
already present in Althusser's original exposition by retreating into a discursive
idealism, Paul Hirst (1979) represents the most telling failure to come to terms
with Althusser's theory of ideology. By not linking Althusser's assertion that
ideology is material to the claim that the subject is constituted through the act of
interpellation, Hirst concludes that Althusser remains within the Cartesian problematic. Hirst argues that Althusser assumes the ability of the individual to recognize itself in order to be interpellated and in this way Althusser, in Cartesian
fashion, defines the subject in terms of cognitive ability.

The dual-mirror relation only works if the subject(s) who recognizes already had the attributes of a knowing subject; the
mirror of the Subject serves as a means of reflection, giving

---

[9] As evident from the quote above, Therborn also tends to fall back to a pre-Marxist understanding of materiality as an issue of substances (as in the materialism of Hobbes, for
example) rather than emphasizing the materiality of social relations.

the subject an *image*, that image is, however, *recognized* by the subject as *its* image. Recognition, the crucial moment of the constitution (activation) of the subject, presupposes a point of cognition prior to the recognition. Something must recognize that which it is to be. (Hirst 1979, 65)

Althusser's analysis of the "mechanism" of ideology describes and reproduces certain of the forms of religious and philosophical theory. Further evidence for this is to be found in the fact that the interpellation relation subject-individual can be placed within Althusser's own empiricism-idealism structure of the subject and the essence without undue violence. The subject which the individual is to be represents the essence, an essence which transcends the "abstract" individual, and the abstract individual represents the "subject," an empty individual with nothing but the facilities necessary to receive the subject that it will be. The empiricism of the "subject" here requires the support of certain prior suppositions (that it is a cognising subject). (Hirst 1979, 67–68)

Hirst's comments in part derive from a reading of Althusser by way of the early use of the concept of the mirror stage. The concept of the mirror stage derives from the "mirror test" developed by Henri Wallon in 1931. The test was used to show the differences between humans and other primates by showing that a six-month-old human is capable of recognizing its own image in a mirror, while a chimpanzee apparently is not (cf. Evans 1996, 115–116). Lacan's concept of the mirror stage specifies the role of the specular image in the function of language as well as the formation of the ego by providing unity, via this recognition, to what otherwise could simply be thought of as a meaningless set of biological parts. Hirst seems to assume that this act of recognition, since it is recognition that creates or "activates" the subject, must presuppose some essence of cognition on the part of the "subject to be." If the intelligibility of images were a simple biological or theological attribute, Hirst would be right.[10] However, this is

---

[10] Surprisingly, Hirst's critique has been accepted with little challenge by many commentators on Althusser. This is the case with Ted Benton (1984), who simply repeats Hirst's comments adding, "the concept of 'interpellation' is no advance over the conception of socialization offered by functionalist sociology" (Benton 1984, 107). The absurdity of this claim is evaluated latter on in this essay. Michael Sprinker takes up Hirst's critique, arguing that recognition is better thought of as a "causal power" rather than a mental faculty (Sprinker 1987, 198). Sprinker's defense of interpellation, however, quickly falls into the same trap as Hirst's critique by arguing that this causal power "is an observable potential of a structure whose nature remains unknown in the present state of research in neurophysiology and cognitive psychology" (Sprinker 1987, 199). In the end, Sprinker simply repeats Hirst's position by treating recognition as presocial, whether as an aspect

not the case. For Lacan, the imaginary is structured by way of the symbolic.[11] The recognition of the image can only come about within an already established matrix or topology of images by way of the symbolic (cf. Žižek 1991, 10–11). As Bruce Fink has noted:

> Such "images" derive from how the parental Other "sees" the child and are thus linguistically structured. Indeed, it is the symbolic order that brings about the internalization of mirror and other images (e.g., photographic images), for it is primarily due to the parents' reaction to such images that they become charged, in the child's eyes, with libidinal interest or value—which is why mirror images are not of great interest to the child prior to about six months of age, in other words, prior to the functioning of language in the child (which occurs well before the child is able to speak). (Fink 1995, 36–37)

The phenomenon of recognition is thus not an a priori assumption, as Hirst argues, but is an attribute of the symbolic order.[12]

Interpellations, then, occur only after the "subject to be" has come to occupy a space in the symbolic order. This is clear from Althusser's often quoted assertion that "the individual is always already a subject."[13] How do we

---

of our biology or not, and thus becomes a presupposition since it is beyond the explanatory powers of the theory itself.

[11] For an elaboration of Lacan's concept of the symbolic and the imaginary, see Jameson (1988, 75–115).

[12] Althusser's definition of ideology as an "imaginary representation" is in this context very misleading, in that it does not correspond to the Lacanian definition of the imaginary order; however, it does not necessarily follow that ideology is simply on the level of the symbolic. As Rastko Mocnik (1993) has argued, ideology operates within both the symbolic and imaginary registers. Mocnik attempted to answer the question of why a particular interpellation is or is not successful by arguing that an utterance acts as its own mirror by registering in the symbolic and imaginary orders concurrently. While this answer is compatible with the answer we will give below, it begs the question of how the symbolic order is constituted and does not examine the role of ideology as practice in this formation of the symbolic order. As can be noted in the discussion of Žižek that follows, the answer to this question that Žižek provides is superior on these issues.

[13] Although this position has often been misunderstood as contradictory to the concept of interpellation (Hirst had viewed it as some essentialist survival in Althusser's theory of ideology), it is best understood in this context of the interpellation occurring only after the individual has come to occupy a space in the symbolic order. The whole of this passage from Althusser is intelligible only in this context: "That an individual is always-already a subject, even before he is born, is nevertheless the plain reality, accessible to everyone and not a paradox at all. Freud shows that individuals are always 'abstract' with respect to the subjects they always-already are, simply by noting the ideological ritual that surrounds the expectation of a 'birth,' that 'happy event.' Everyone knows how much and in what way an unborn child is expected. Which amounts to saying, if we agree

reconcile this position, however, with the argument that ideology is material? Certainly, simply by noting the centrality of the symbolic order in interpellations, we have done little to overcome the problem of discursive idealism.

Slavoj Žižek (1989, 11–53) has done the most to overcome this uncertainty between interpellation and ideology. Žižek not only correctly identifies Althusser's lack of clarity regarding the relation between ideology and interpellation, but also highlights Althusser's use of Pascal.[14] Žižek restates the radical message of Althusser's conception of ideology as practice and helps to resolve the question of why certain interpellations take place. Counter to Montag (1996), we can say that this revival of the radical and subversive in Althusser is due precisely to the reading of Althusser with the help of Lacan and Pascal. While others reduce Althusser's theory of ideology to a discursive idealism, Žižek emphasizes the role of practice and ritual. Two quotes from Pascal are most relevant:

---

to drop the 'sentiments,' i.e., the forms of family ideology (paternal/maternal/conjugal /fraternal) in which the unborn child is expected: it is certain in advance that it will bear its Father's Name, and will therefore have an identity and be irreplaceable. Before its birth, the child is therefore always-already a subject, appointed as a subject in and by the specific familial ideological configuration in which it is 'expected' once it has been conceived" (Althusser 1971, 176).

A related issue is the role of misrecognition in interpellations. The subject necessarily misrecognizes that it is the act the interpellation that makes it the identity it has recognized itself as. Thus, the subject is "always already" what it recognizes itself as from the point of view of its own consciousness.

[14] Warren Montag (1996) has gone so far as to assert that Althusser's use of Pascal is most un-Pascalian, in that he does not maintain the presumed mind-body dualism of Pascal in favor of a Spinozist combining of the two. He also argues that it is impossible to reconstruct Althusser's theory of ideology by way of psychoanalysis: "there is no longer any question of 'correcting' or completing Althusser's essay with the aid of Lacanian theory, given that theory's own impasses and fragmentation" (Montag 1996, 93). Montag never justifies either point; he goes on to argue that it is by way of Hobbes that we can come to terms with Althusser's theory of ideology. He argues that it is Hobbes who shows us how ISA's function, since it is he who first notes the necessity of separating the masses into individuals and the necessity for these individuals to "freely" submit to the state or law by way of the "social contract." If we are to judge Montag's reading by its contribution to the theory of ideology, we must conclude that it is of little interest since what he does say about individualization had already been said by Poulantzas in his discussion of the "isolation effect" (1973), and, although he gives an interesting reading of Hobbes by way of Althusser, his use of Hobbes does not shed any light on the possible ways interpellations may actually function.

It is interesting to note the fetishism presupposed by Hobbes' discussion of the social contract. The social contract does not refer to any real event, it need only refer to how men must act in order for the state to gain sovereignty: "men must act *as if* they had moved out of a state of nature by agreement (emphasis in original; Macpherson 1962, 20)."

> You want to be cured of unbelief and you ask for the remedy:
> learn from those who were once bound like you and who now
> wager all they have . . . They behaved just as if they did be-
> lieve, taking holy water, having masses said, and so on. That
> will make you believe quite naturally, and will make you more
> docile. (Pascal 1995, 125)[15]

> For we must make no mistake about ourselves: we are as
> much automation as mind . . . How few things can be demon-
> strated! Proofs only convince the mind; habit provides the
> strongest proofs and those that are most believed. It inclines
> the automation, which leads the mind unconsciously along
> with it. (Pascal 1995, 247)

Recall Althusser's position that "recognition only gives us the "consciousness"
of our incessant (eternal) practice of ideological recognition" (Althusser 1971,
173). This position adheres to Pascal's privileging of practice over consciousness. We can say that interpellations and beliefs only come about once they have
already occurred on the level of practice. Ideology in this way is practice, and
based upon the content of such practices and their repetitions (ritualization) a
given identity or belief will arise on the level of the subject's consciousness. In
Balibar's words, "the subject is practice" (1995, 25). Žižek notes the difference
between this position and that of behaviorism, and establishes why Benton's
(1984) assertion that Althusser's theory of interpellation is no advance over
functionalist theories of socialization is misguided:

> What distinguishes this Pascalian "custom" from insipid be-
> haviourist wisdom ("the content of your belief is conditioned
> by your factual behavior") is the paradoxical status of a *belief*
> *before belief*: by following a custom, the subject believes
> without knowing it, so that the final conversion is merely a
> formal act by means of which we recognize what we have al-
> ready believed. (Žižek 1989, 40)

Žižek helps clarify the link between ideology and interpellation, but
does not fully explain it. Are many beliefs or identities possible from the same
practices or customs? How is the ideological content of practices determined?
Given the science/ideology distinction Althusser uses, we can say that practices
are ideological because they are experienced. All experience is ideology; science
begins when we depart from experience into abstract categories that do not presuppose the subject, the I. To paraphrase Althusser, science is a subjectless dis-

---

[15] Althusser's paraphrase "Kneel down, move your lips in prayer, and you will believe" is
likely derived from this passage.

course (Althusser 1971, 173).[16] Since experience is always from the perspective of the I, experience does not exist until the subject exists. Prior to interpellation, there is no experience or practices to serve as its basis. In historical time, the practices occur before the interpellation, but the experience or meaning of these practices can only be established once the interpellation has occurred. Here interpellation, as effect, precedes its cause.

It is Pêcheux and Žižek who again do the most to explain this element in Althusser's thought. Pêcheux termed this paradox the "Munchausen Effect"— the paradox of the subject being the "cause of himself" (Pêcheux 1982, 103– 109). Discussing Althusser's definition of interpellation, Pêcheux notes that:

> the formulation carefully avoids presupposing the existence of the subject on whom the operation of interpellation is per- formed—it does not say: "The subject is interpellated by Ide- ology." . . . The paradox is precisely that interpellation has, as it were, a *retroactive effect*. (Pêcheux 1982, 106)

The retroactive effect (or, more properly, the retroactive cause) is this "Mun- chausen Effect." This is emphasized in Žižek's discussion of dialectics in psy- choanalysis, and here we see the homology between Althusser's theory of ideol- ogy and psychoanalytic practice (cf. Žižek 1989, 55–69). The repressed (uncon- scious) cause of a given symptom only arises after the symptom.

> The Lacanian answer to the question: From where does the re- pressed return? is therefore, paradoxically: From the future. Symptoms are meaningless traces, their meaning not discov- ered, excavated from the hidden depth of the past, but con- structed retroactively—the analysis produces the truth; that is, the signifying frame which gives the symptoms their symbolic place and meaning. (Žižek 1989, 55–56)

This perfectly describes the dialectical relation between ideological practice and interpellation. It is the interpellation that gives meaning (ideological content) to the practices that, in turn, are the cause of the interpellation. While a discursive idealism (as found in Laclau et al.) is to be avoided, so too is a strict determin- ism of practices over thought (which a narrow reading of Pascal might imply). Practices have no inherent meaning or causal weight in and of themselves. Only after they are incorporated into a symbolic order (which occurs when the indi-

---

[16] The origin and philosophical foundations of this distinction can be found in the work of Gaston Bachelard, Althusser's mentor (cf. Bachelard 1984 and Tiles 1984). Gregory Elliott has noted that this distinction is also in line with the Spinozist influence on Al- thusser, "with its [Spinoza's rationalism] total differentiation between rational knowledge and the 'opinion' or 'imagination' derived from random sense experience" (Elliott 1987, 53).

vidual is interpellated as a subject) do they acquire any causal weight.[17] The ideological content of a given set of practices will vary according to the symbolic order they are embedded within.[18] For an interpellation to be successful, it must base itself on a given set of material supports that acquire their causal weight with the interpellation.

Let us take the interpellation "sinner" as an illustrative example. A young child may engage in the practices associated with "praying" without attaching any meaning to them; they are simply empty rituals. The bowing of a head, or kneeling, or placing one's hands together need not have any religious or moral meaning (it is hard to imagine a child of two thinking of himself as a sinner). At a later point in time the child may recognize himself as a "sinner" in the discourse of the religious Subject (the religious big Other or symbolic order). What were once empty practices now become the material/ideological cause of the interpellation since praying only makes sense if one assumes the position of "sinner." The identity "sinner" was already presupposed by the practice of praying, even though the child was unaware of this at the time. The point of becoming conscious of the belief that one is a sinner (the moment of interpellation) coincides with the attribution of religious meaning to the past experience of "praying." Of course, if a "sinner" is asked when it is that he became a sinner he will surely not answer "when I was interpellated as such" and will likely respond that he has always been a sinner (born with original sin). Here we see that only by reference to the symbolic order can we attribute ideological content to practices and that these practices can indeed represent "belief before belief."

Through this reformulation of Althusser's theory of ideology we are able to overcome the problems with Althusser's exposition, but the actual use of the theory to examine the production of national subjects must overcome two remaining problems. We must be able to distinguish respective hierarchies of identities and practices. As noted in the review of Easton, the identification as a national subject must be strong enough to displace competing identifications. Individuals are subject to multiple interpellations. Someone may be concurrently American, Republican, Texan, teacher, Christian, white, and mother; but for national identities to be fully functional (producing national political communi-

---

[17] This point brings us back to the role of misrecognition in interpellation. As argued before, there is a necessary misrecognition that occurs during the interpellation because for the individual to be interpellated as a subject she must misrecognize that it is the interpellation that makes her into a subject. The subject must misrecognize that the present (interpellation) has brought about the past (her belief that she was already what she recognizes herself as); as the Lacanian dictum puts it, "the truth arises out of misrecognition."

[18] Luckily, in social analysis we are always looking backward, so the indeterminacy and play between ideology and interpellation do not present a problem, since we will already know if the interpellation occurred and the ideological practices present at the time. This dialectical relation, of course, does make it difficult to predict if a certain interpellation will be successful, since we cannot be sure of the ideological content that will be attributed to a given set of practices before an interpellation actually happens.

ties and state legitimacy) they must be able to supersede other identities. Nothing we have discussed so far and nothing in Althusser allow us to explain how this may be accomplished. Concurrently, if all we know is that interpellations are a product of the ideological content of practices and of (mis)recognition, we are faced with an almost infinite set of practices within everyday life to draw upon in any attempt to explain a particular interpellation.[19] Althusser does help us on this matter with his discussion of ideological state apparatuses. Althusser emphasizes the role of the educational apparatus as most important followed by the family, media, and so on. Indeed, there is now a significant body of Althusserian analysis on education and other ideological apparatuses. However, the analysis of Ideological State Apparatuses (ISAs) does not fully answer this problem of a hierarchy of practices. The section below argues that the ISA is a confusing category, given Althusser's own use of ideology and interpellation, and an alternative category is proposed by way of psychoanalysis and Henri Lefebvre.

Enjoyment and the Everyday

Reality shows us that civilization is not content with the ties we have so far allowed it. It aims at binding the members of the community together in a libidinal way as well and employs every means to that end. It favors every path by which strong identifications can be established between the community, and it summons up aim-inhibited libido on the largest scale so as to strengthen the communal bond.

—Sigmund Freud, *Civilization and Its Discontents*

The short answer to our remaining problems can be found in psychoanalysis. Identities possess libidinal value. There can be a hierarchy of identities by virtue of their libidinal content. Similarly, the practices that cause such libido-infested interpellations would be identifiable by virtue of their libidinal attraction.

If we examine the political and ethical implications of Althusser's theory of ideology, the need for an understanding of the libidinal content of identities becomes clear. For Althusser, our identities are symptoms of our social existence; they are omnipresent and necessary. As long as society exists, so will ideology and identities.[20] This is the basis for Althusser's reproach that the

---

[19] A similar problem was identified by Poulantzas (1966) in relation to Althusser's concept of overdetermination. Poulantzas argued that the concept was not able to distinguish between a hierarchy of determinations and could very well lead to endless description rather than focused analysis.

[20] All identities are in this way alienating since individuals will be interpellated as subjects and thus misrecognize themselves as something they are not (alienation). What someone really is would, in this context, be beyond all particular identities. The Lacanian

concept of alienation is ideological and pre-Marxist. Since alienation is universal and not particular to capitalism, its elimination is impossible and cannot be a revolutionary goal.[21] The political position implied in Althusser is one of a critical self-awareness of our own identities as symptoms, misrecognitions, effects of our social being. Although we cannot avoid alienation we can curb its delusional effects through an understanding of the mechanism of interpellation. However, even if we are aware of the ideological causes of our identities, we may not be able to liberate ourselves from them. Symptoms may continue even after their causes are uncovered if the symptoms contain libidinal value (cf. Žižek 1989, ch. 2).[22] Even if we explain to an "American" that her identity as such is only a misrecognition, that she is not really an "American," that her ability to think critically is limited by this misrecognition, we are not likely to succeed in "curing" her if her identification as American is a source of enjoyment.[23]

The libidinal contents of identities are evident through "pertinent effects" (cf. Poulantzas 1973, 79–84). Obviously, the libidinal value of an identity is radically contingent (i.e., the identity "Marxist" may have a very strong or very weak attraction). The Poulantzasian concept of pertinent effects helps us on this issue; the existence of class struggle is revealed by its effects, "pertinent effects" because only by way of class struggle could such effects be produced. The only way we can know of the presence and amount of libidinal value in a particular identity is through its pertinent effects; for example, the response provoked by the burning of a national flag. If no one reacts, it is safe to say that at that time the given national identity does not have a high libidinal value; if there is a strong response, we can say that the identity does have a high libidinal

---

definition of a fool (someone who really thinks he is what he is for someone else) applies to this case.

[21] In Marx we find at least two different uses of the term alienation. At times (the more traditional use of the term) it refers to the physical separation of a product of labor from its producer, and at times it refers to the misrecognition that occurs because of the commodity form. For example, in the *Economic and Philosophical Manuscripts* we find both uses; at times it refers to exploitation and at times it refers to the alienation of man from himself (by misrecognizing himself as a commodity), from society (by misrecognizing relations between himself and other people as a relation between himself and things/commodities), and from nature (by misrecognizing his interaction with nature as an interaction with commodities) (cf. Marx 1992, 322–334). It is obviously to the latter use of alienation that Althusser's critique is directed.

[22] Cornell West (1994, 35–49) illustrates this point well in his essay "The Pitfalls of Racial Reasoning." West's critique of the use of racial identities as epistemic categories fits very well with the Althusserian critique of identities; his proposed solution, unfortunately, does not take into account the libidinal value of identities and presents "moral reasoning" as something we should choose over "racial reasoning" without any real analysis of how someone could make such a "choice" and the parameters of such agency.

[23] A "just say no" approach to nationalism or racism will not work any better than it did for drug abuse.

value. In contemporary society national identities have a significant degree of libidinal value; the pertinent effects are countless and obvious.

How do identities come to possess libidinal value? Although it may be easy to know if identities have a libidinal value, how these values are allocated is not at all evident. As already noted, identities have two elements: the ideological practices that function as their cause and the position within the symbolic order they signify. The loci of the libidinal value may be either of the two or both. If we look to ideological practices, it is easy to understand based upon our own experiences that a drink at the corner bar, the viewing of a sports event, or the writing of a poem may be a source of satisfaction. This experience is easy enough to explain by way of Freud's discussion of the sublimation of the libido into socially acceptable activities (cf. Freud 1960). But we are unable to know which acceptable practices are attributable to a given identity without first knowing its position within the symbolic order. The libidinal value of a given practice is not a function of its "essence" (watching baseball is not universally enjoyable), but it acquires value through the meanings attached to it by the symbolic order.

To further complicate matters, identities may often be floating, as in the case of populist projects. The same identity can come to represent many different and conflicting sets of practices. Identities need not refer to any characteristics. The term "middle American" may refer to a gay Jewish New York lawyer just as easily as to a fundamentalist Christian potato farmer. Here, what one is identifying with is not a set of characteristics but a symbolic position, a point of view. We can thus speak of two kinds of identifications: imaginary and symbolic (Žižek 1989, 105–107).[24] Imaginary identities are identifications with an image (the reflection in the mirror stage). The identity as "mother" or "student" or "worker" is imaginary to the degree that one identifies with a set of characteristics that constitutes our image of that identity. Symbolic identities are identifications with the place from where these images are being viewed, the symbolic position that attaches meaning to the image (the gaze of the parental Other in the mirror stage). Interpellations are thus constituted by two imperatives: to identify with a particular image and to assume the symbolic position from which that image is viewed (to take on a certain subjectivity).[25]

---

[24] This point brings us back to the role of the imaginary and the symbolic in interpellations.

[25] Interpellations are dominating for this reason, since we not only are compelled to conform to the image projected by this symbolic Other but also are compelled to identify with the symbolic position itself. As Lacan puts it, "the subject is subject only from being subjected to the field of the Other" (Lacan 1981, 188). This point is freely admitted when discussing, for example, the image of beauty in the media but is almost never noted in discussions of nationality or family or work or any other significant source of identity. Our domination by national, religious, and familial identities is seldom recognized. That the slogan of the Greek Junta was "Nation, Religion, Family" is not surprising.

This point of symbolic identification produces a suturing or organizing effect on the field of practices. Practices possess libidinal value by virtue of their organization by the symbolic order. Let us take as an example the slogan "Baseball, Hot Dogs, Apple Pie, and Chevrolet." What is being asked of the consumer? To identify with an image of Chevrolet?[26] To identify Chevrolet as American? The advertisement implores the consumer to view Chevrolet from the same symbolic position from which the other objects appear as belonging together; to view a Chevrolet through American eyes. It implies that only in this way can the true meaning or significance of Chevrolet be understood. A Chevrolet cannot be reduced to the sum of its physical parts. It is a materialization of the elusive American way, the American essence manifest in baseball and hot dogs. In this context the identity "American" cannot be reduced to any characteristics (it is not simply an imaginary identity) but is a position from which a cluster of practices derives its meaning or unity.

What is this essence that is manifest in both hot dogs and apple pies? What is that part of Chevrolet that unites it with these things? Common to all these objects is that "Americans" enjoy them all; that which unites hot dogs and Chevrolet is that they are manifestations of a particularly American way of enjoying.[27] Here, the dialectical relation between symbolic identities and their articulations within the field of practices becomes clear: the symbolic identification is necessary for the organization of practices, but the compelling force behind the identification is the practices themselves.[28]

> The element which holds together a given community cannot
> be reduced to the point of symbolic identification: the bond
> linking together its members always implies a shared relation
> to a Thing, toward Enjoyment incarnated . . . If we are asked
> how we can recognize the presence of this Thing, the only
> consistent answer is that the Thing is present in that elusive
> entity called "our way of life." All we can do is enumerate
> disconnected fragments of the way our community organizes
> its feasts, its rituals of mating, its initiation ceremonies, in
> short, all the details by which is made visible the unique way a

---

[26] As with the slogan for Mercury, "Imagine Yourself in a Mercury."

[27] From this point on I will tend to use the Lacanian term *enjoyment* (*jouissance*) rather than the more general terms *libido* and *pleasure*. While there are differences between Freud's use of pleasure and Lacan's use of enjoyment, enjoyment refers to the pleasure one derives from denying oneself pleasure (cf. Lacan 1992), and although this represents a recasting of the concept of libido (a term Lacan almost never uses), either term is acceptable for the rather loose formulations presented here (my use of psychoanalytic concepts should be seen as a selective appropriation rather than a rigorous exposition). I prefer the term enjoyment only in order to be consistent with the terminology of the secondary sources I am using.

[28] Here we return again to the cause-effect inversion identified earlier.

community *organizes its enjoyment.* . . . The national Cause is ultimately nothing but the way subjects of a given ethnic community organize their enjoyment through national myths. (Žižek 1993, 201–202)

As Žižek notes, the level of practice is what gives causal weight and substance to the discursive/symbolic order.[29] Echoes of Pascal abound; he could have easily said "move your lips in song, eat your hot dog, drive your Chevy, and you will believe as an American." On a practical level, most people are aware that the organization of enjoyment differentiates national communities. Typical American statements on how they are different from other nationalities may include claims that the French smell, Mexicans are lazy, Japanese work too much, and so on. For all the similarities between the Americans and the English, the real distance between them can be typically seen in Manhattan pubs that televise games during English soccer season, often packed with British expatriates cheering and shouting and debating to the amusement and incomprehension of the American patrons.[30]

   In his analysis of the national cause, Žižek tends to emphasize national myths and narratives in the organization of enjoyment as a national enjoyment (cf. Žižek 1993, 200–237). Although looking to myths and narratives enables us to examine the function of national historiography and other fantasies in the production of national communities, it tends to undertheorize the role of everyday practices (Žižek does make frequent use of them as illustrative examples). At other points, he recognizes the role of the nation-state, beyond its various myths and narratives, as the "predominant frame of identification with the ethnic Thing" (Žižek 1994, 79). The question is, how are we to know if a given practice is part of a national enjoyment? If we emphasize the role of national myths, festivals, and rites, we are limited to a fairly small group of practices self-identified by their overt nationalist content (e.g., Independence Day parades, John Wayne movies, and voting). I do not think we can limit ourselves to these overtly nationalistic practices, and the conceptual logic of what we have discussed so far, as well as Žižek's analysis, indicates that the more banal everyday

---

[29] In addition to the symbolic and imaginary orders, Žižek is here making reference to the Lacanian Real (that which resists symbolization, the excess or surplus that remains outside the symbolic order). Our enjoyment itself produces an excess that we are unable to reconcile into the symbolic order; the Thing is the Real Thing: it is elusive since we can never reduce it to symbolization and it functions as object-cause of desire.

[30] The stereotypical image of the "ugly American" tourist fits this dynamic; what is being alluded to is their "ugly" relation to enjoyment (clothes, food, etc.) compared to the native forms of enjoyment. In Greece, English tourists are ridiculed for their inability to enjoy alcohol properly. The Greek tradition of drinking and eating together is contrasted to the English style of drinking excessive amounts while not eating, with the resulting tendency of English tourists to be less than sober.

practices are of vital importance.[31] After all, what could be more American than apple pie? As already noted, practices will gain meaning and unity by virtue of the symbolic position they are being viewed from. Just as no given practice is inherently enjoyable, so no practice is inherently national, or ethnic, or local, or global. The analysis of practices and enjoyment is inherently a phenomenological exercise. The only way we can know if a given practice occupies a position within this national relation to enjoyment is by knowing if people experience this practice as such. To explain why and how the organization of enjoyment occurs is one thing; to identify and describe it is another.[32]

The place we must look to in order to identify what practices are operant in the production of the national community is everyday life. Althusser's Ideological State Apparatuses (ISAs) must be replaced by Lefebvre's everyday life. If we were to do a strict Althusserian analysis we would look to the schools, the family, and other bureaucracies as the loci of these ideological practices that interpellate individuals as national subjects. The problem with this approach lies in the use of the terms "state" and "apparatuses." In speaking of "state," Althusser implies that ideology only has state functions or expands the definition of the state to be everything and everywhere. Althusser's own definition of ideology would preclude such a possibility since it is universal and could not be reduced to any particular (national or state) ideology. In addition, he would readily admit that the state is a historical particular and not universal. By using the term "apparatus," he implies a kind of formal unity of the practices within these institutions based on the quasi-legalistic demarcation of "family," "school," and "labor union." Any taxonomy that tends to correspond to the various ministries of a Western state is suspect. The unity of practices must be established, not assumed, and the tendency to reproduce formal/legal categories as analytical categories must be resisted. Indeed, it could be easily argued using Althusser's own theory that these categories themselves are ideological effects grounded on our experiences rather than on our causal understanding of social phenomenon. Everyday life is a useful alternative to ISAs for two reasons: first, it does not assume any formal or legal distinctions within the totality of practices constitutive of the everyday; second, it stresses the ritualistic and repetitive aspects of these practices. Everyday life is a historical category, corresponding to the particular temporal organization of life into repetitive twenty-four-hour units (cf. Lefebvre 1971 and 1991, ch. 1). Practices are repeated, life has a mechanistic quality, and, for this reason, everyday life is dominating, boring, and undesirable. Lefebvre's analysis corresponds perfectly with Pascal's and Althusser's discussions of custom and ritual. It is not simply practices, but the habituation of

---

[31] See Michael Billig (1995) on the everyday manifestations of nationalism.

[32] The methodological example for this kind of analysis is Marx's analysis of the commodity form. The contingency of the commodity form must first be described on the level of appearances before we can have a causal understanding of the necessity of that appearance given existing social relations. We must first understand how a practice is experienced before we can explain the cause and function of this experience.

practices, "material practices governed by material rituals" (Althusser 1971, 170), that "leads the mind unconsciously with it" (Pascal).[33] Everyday life can be the only loci of ideological practices.

Within this so far undifferentiated continuum of ideological practices qua everyday life, we will need to make substantive differentiations in order to establish a causal hierarchy of practices as they relate to a particular interpellation. Replacing "state" with "national enjoyment" stresses the point that the unity of any set of ideological practices are not formal or a priori but are overdetermined by their relation to each other from the point of view of the effect/product we are trying to explain: a unity of otherwise contingent practices when viewed from the position of an ideological effect (in our case, the national individual).[34] For example, eating apple pies and driving a Chevy are contingent, unless we view them from the perspective of the American national identity and the complex totality of practices that function to support this interpellation.

Replacing "apparatus" with "everyday life" makes explicit, first, the inability to reduce the function of ideology to any intentionality (state or otherwise) and, second, that ideological practices function in an automated and self-referential way. Self-referential based on this overdetermined unity since only in the complex relation of practices to each other and to the symbolic order do they acquire any ideological weight and automated because their functioning presupposes no intentionality on the part of those who may have instituted them or those who are experiencing them. An apparatus (like a hammer or an artificial limb) implies a subject who is directing it or using it. Althusser's essay can thus be easily misread to imply that the state or bourgeoisie is "behind" or controls ideological practices. While it is no doubt true that the law or the priests or the parents or the teachers may sanction or institute practices, their ideological function cannot be legislated or willed by them. Overdetermined is the same as underdetermined: the existence of a practice is never a sufficient condition for its ideological function. The complexity and contingency of the relations between the various practices that unify them and give them causal weight are thus a complex process of the various parts interacting as a whole and having definite, automated effects that cannot be reduced to any one part or any one will.[35] The failure of the Cultural Revolution is an example of this process. Neither Mao nor manual labor could control the complex autopoetic workings of what Althusser could have termed the "spontaneous ideology" of the student revolutionaries.

---

[33] There are obvious similarities between this position and Bourdieu's concept of habitus, even though references to Lefebvre are conspicuously absent in his work and he is surprisingly quick to ridicule Althusser (cf. Bourdieu 1990, 52–80).

[34] We can only say that ideological practices are "belief before belief" once we know the "after" of this "before."

[35] This point is already present in the previous discussions of the dialectical relation between practices and interpellations and the impossibility of predicting the ideological content of a practice before the interpellation.

The value of the Althusserian approach to questions of ethnic and national identity remains to be realized, given the lack of empirical research within
this problematic. The need for empirical research is twofold: it will help refine
our abstract understanding of the mechanisms at work in the interpellation process, and it will help us identify those everyday practices that play a central role
in the making of the national individual (as well as other identities). The analytical and political importance of this understanding is significant since we will be
able to identify and explain the practices at work in the process of the social
production of the national individual. As noted above, any understanding of the
real working of interpellation presupposes a knowledge of the everyday routines
of individuals and how they experience them. An Althusserian phenomenology
of our everyday routines is what must be produced, and substantive research into
the vicissitudes of the play between these practices and the symbolic order is
needed. The following chapter, an examination of the everyday practices at
work in the contemporary production of the Greek American interpellation, is an
attempt to both illustrate the analytical utility of the theoretical concepts developed in this chapter and to begin the process of identifying these nationalist everyday practices. It is a beginning for empirical studies that rely upon the concept
of interpellation to explain identity. "Greek Americans" will be studied as a kind
of subgroup or mode of "Americans," and the process of national individualization as it is presently constituted in New York City's Greek American community will be examined.

5

The Constitution of the Greek Americans: Toward an Empirical Study of Interpellation

> The little strains of daily life will support him in his decisive discovery more than great intellectual convulsions will. Having first eaten *couscous* with curiosity, he now tastes it from time to time out of politeness and finds that "it's filling, it's degrading and it's not nourishing." It is "torture by suffocation," he says humorously. Or if he does like *couscous*, he cannot stand the "fairground music" which seizes and deafens him each time he passes a cafe. "Why so loud? How can they hear each other?" He is tortured by that odor of mutton fat which stinks up many of the houses. Many traits of the colonized shock or irritate him. He is unable to conceal the revulsions he feels and which manifest themselves in remarks which strangely recall those of a colonialist.
>
> —Albert Memmi, *The Colonizer and the Colonized*

Memmi's description of how even well-intentioned, leftist, nonnative residents of colonies come to despise and look down upon the native cultures and peoples is striking. More important than "intellectual convulsions" are all those forms of enjoyment that come to mark the real distance between colonizer and colonized. Memmi's argument regarding how everyday life in the colonies transforms even the most well-intentioned nonnative into a colonizing subject rests upon the differing organization of enjoyment constitutive of the colonizer and the colonized. Nonnatives not only may bring with them an intellectual conviction regarding the virtues, fundamental equality, and unjustified domination of the colonized, they also bring with them all the routines and habits of the colonial center. Moreover, they also carry with them the symbolic order of the colonial center with all its categorizations and typologies. Only in relation to an already constituted and interpellated subject from the colonial center do couscous and "fairground music" appear as enjoyments that are somehow anomalous and inferior. Similarly, the real weight of these "little strains of daily life" is not simply a function of categorizing them as "foreign" and anomalous but is very much dependent upon the enjoyment operant within those practices that the colonizing subject is accustomed to.

The purpose of this chapter is to illustrate how the conceptual insights of the previous chapter can be used to explain how national identity is founded upon everyday practices. Rather than try to formulate some general explanation of the "American" national identity, this chapter will focus on one of its subdivisions, the Greek American identity. The reason behind this is the heterogeneous character of everyday life in the United States; the differences in everyday practices depending upon geographical location, social class, ethnicity, and so on, preclude anything approaching a single and homogenous everyday foundation of the American national identity. It may be the case that there are some everyday practices that "Americans" of all the various subclassifications will tend to find enjoyable and categorize as "American." At this point, given the absence of the requisite empirical studies, we can only guess as to if such universally "American" practices exist and, if so, what they are. What we do know is that a great many individuals who reside in the United States do tend to identify along ethnic-national lines: Italian Americans, African American, Irish Americans, and so on. We also know that it is a characteristic of the American national identity that "Americanness" is constituted by such diversity, much like the typical ethnic makeup of military units in American war movies (usually containing someone black, Jewish, Italian, a New Yorker, a Californian, someone from an agricultural small town, and so on, all united and equal in their Americanness). In this way, those who identify as "Americans" typically do so based upon their particular place within the symbolic and everyday spaces of American society.

Much like the example Memmi provides us with, the goal will be to understand how individuals who have been interpellated as Greek Americans experience and categorize everyday practices that may serve as cause of the interpellation. The few interviews that the following discussion is based upon are of college students in New York City who identify as Greek American. These are not nearly enough interviews in terms of absolute numbers and in terms of the diversity of the interviewees to provide some conclusive or authoritative explanation of the Greek American identity, although this initial analysis may prove to be suggestive and help guide future efforts to produce more complete explanations. As already noted, the goals of this chapter are much more modest. This brief case study of the Greek American identity is an experiment to see if the conceptual framework outlined in the previous chapter is up to the empirical challenge of explaining interpellations as a product of everyday practices and to see how the concepts can be operationalized for the systematic empirical study of the foundations of the national political community.

The data from the interviews have been organized into sections corresponding to different areas of everyday life. In each of these sections below, those practices that seem to be of libidinal value are identified and the ways that they are categorized and experienced by the subjects are noted. In the section following the descriptions, these practices as a totality are discussed, and, based upon the patterns in the ways that the practices are categorized, the symbolic order that maps and gives a national meaning to these practices is deduced and discussed. In the concluding section, the implications of this initial empirical exploration towards the theories of the previous chapter and toward future empirical research are discussed.

The Fried and the Baked

A significant ensemble of everyday practices and sources of enjoyment entails food and eating. What are those foods and eating practices that Greek Americans enjoy, and how do they categorize and organize these practices along ethnic-national lines? A significant distinction seems to be that of Greek American food as opposed to Greek and American foods. There is a tendency to identify "American" food as that which is fast and convenient; as one of the interviewed noted, "Your chicken patties, your quesadillas, ready food, quick food, fast food." Similarly, American food was also equated with "finger food" and foods that don't involve a lot of sauces and ingredients: steaks, chicken fingers, and buffalo wings. Concurrent with this distinction is the idea that Greek food is somehow more wholesome and involves more time and preparation; the culinary talents of the Greek mother were also often noted, and it seems that almost everyone believes his/her mother to be a great cook.

Within the domain of "Greek" foods we also find a clear distinction between what differentiates Greek and Greek American foods. Greek American food is different not so much because of any differences in actual ingredients and style but because of the differences in quantities. The cheese pies in New York are huge, it is noted, when compared to those found in Greece: "At Athens Cafe the cheese pies are bigger than the plate. The corners are sticking out of your plate." A similar distinction is noted when it comes to gyros and *souvlakia* (like a gyro but with cubes of meat, usually pork, rather than strips of or minced meat). While some stated that the gyros in Greece are more tasty, the descriptions of eating the American versions are very direct regarding the enjoyment derived from them, "Big sandwich, you don't know where to start, you attempt to eat it and it falls apart, it gets messy, the grease runs all down your hands." The enjoyment operant from the excess of the size itself is purely American: the gyro is so big that it is hard to handle, the grease runs down your hands, it is messy, probably not too good for you, but, nonetheless, very pleasurable. As one person noted, "Who doesn't like fast food, but I try to avoid it." The same kind of food they would categorize as relatively wholesome (if only because of the size difference) and better prepared (because of the belief in the greater authenticity of the process) in Greece is understood as "fast food" in the United States and inherently more enjoyable to them than the versions found in Greece.

The Discrete Charm of the Greek Americans

When it comes to manners, politics, and cultural attitudes, Greek Americans view themselves as decidedly gentile. All the interviewees noted that Greeks in Greece tend to be rude and obnoxious, especially when it comes to Greek Americans. "The Greeks think we are naive and stupid. They only want our dol-

lars when we go there." The typical Greek quality of *filotimo* (a notoriously difficult term to translate, it refers to the hospitality Greeks have toward others) is
seen as increasingly lacking among Greeks in Greece, explained by their increasing Europeanization. By contrast, Greek Americans see themselves as
much more authentic practitioners of *filotimo* precisely because they do not live
in Greece and are able to retain this traditional virtue.

The gentile character of the Greek Americans is embodied in a wide
range of practices. Bad service from retail clerks, waiters, and bureaucrats was
noted and contrasted to the polite and proper service found in the United States.
Also of importance was the lack of political correctness by Greeks in Greece; a
few stories were told regarding comments Greeks would make regarding the
physical characteristics and appearance of tourists and passersby. All the interviewees found Greek attitudes toward politics and political discussion particularly disturbing. "I don't understand why they were so angry at me. Don't they
understand that Clinton bombed the Serbs, not me? They get too emotional
about these things." Heated and antagonistic political debates were described as
common to the Greeks but as something that the Greek Americans found dis-
tasteful. Much preferred was the more "American" practice of either not discussing politics at all or discussing it in more detached ways. Alternatively, and this
is obviously a function of those interviewed being New York City natives, the
interviewees saw themselves as being more refined and "American" than most
Americans because they live in New York City and are thus much more in tune
with and respectful of the multicultural nature of American society than Americans who live in places like "Montana and Oklahoma." Similarly, when asked
about the attitudes toward Greek Americans by other Americans, all responded
that Greeks are well liked and respected. They partly attributed this to the
friendly and good-natured ways of the Greek Americans and the lack of any
negative characteristics of Greeks in America. As one person responded, "Can I
be a little bit racist? I mean, when you watch the news it is always some black or
Hispanic that creates problems and crime, never the Greeks. So what do Greek
Americans do for others not to like them?" In this way, the Greek Americans
pride themselves on being polite, culturally sensitive, and relatively urbane
when compared with the images they have of some Americans and Greeks.

The Greek American Work Ethic and Family Life

Family life and the working day both seem to be important sources of enjoyment. When it comes to Greek American family practices, the closeness of the
family is often noted. What is interesting are the ways that this closeness is demonstrated. The best expression of the closeness of the Greek American family
supposedly lays in the fact that Greek American parents never charge their children rent. "With most Americans, when their children become eighteen years
old, they either throw them out of the house or charge them rent." Although it
was noted that some other ethnic groups share this family closeness, primarily
Italian Americans, Greek Americans experience parental altruism as a "Greek

American" characteristic and source of pride and satisfaction. Concurrently, they view the work ethic as also being a product of family life and something that distinguishes them from the Greeks. Although paying rent to one's parents is attributed to the anomalous "Americans," the degree to which Greeks rely upon their parents is also seen as being undesirable. It was noted that Greek Americans are much more appreciative of higher education and of the virtues of work than are the Greeks because of the tendency of Greek Americans to work, even while they are students. "I think we are much more dedicated to education. I mean, in Greece they don't even go to classes much and no one ever works. They just sit around drinking coffee and they let their parents feed them. All of us here not only go to school, we also work. We are more serious students." The tendency to have a job seems to be a significant point of libidinal satisfaction, and this is also taken as a sign that Greek Americans are more serious as students. A similar distinction is made regarding the tendency of Greeks to not work after they graduate, "They will just live at home with their parents until they find a job they like. We here will do all kinds of jobs even if we don't like it because we do not see work as a bad thing."

Religion, Superstitions, and Totems

The repetitions and rituals associated with religion and superstitions appear to be of some libidinal value. All the interviewees stated that they do not attend church services. When questioned further, all noted that they go for Easter and Christmas but that it does not count since going for these occasions is more a function of the ethnic culture rather than anything having to do with religious beliefs. None of the interviewees were attempting to hide their attendance; they took it as a given that everyone attends services on these days. All those interviewed wore some sort of religious or quasireligious jewelry (either a cross or a blue stone, used to protect against the "evil eye"). All also tended to place a stone to protect against the "evil eye" in their car and displayed the Greek flag on some part of their car as well (a practice that is extremely common). The one partial exception to this was one person who removed the "evil eye" protector from her car after a string of accidents and since then has had no accidents. When asked if maybe the stone was bad luck, she said that she was certain it was only coincidence, but she decided to do away with it nonetheless.

All those interviewed also noted the pleasures of the religious ceremonies themselves: the chanting, the smell of the incense, the taste of the bread given out during mass, the cathartic feelings that stem from confession, and the feeling of community that religious gatherings foster.[1] This was consistently understood as not being a function of religiosity but of aesthetics. "I like going

---

[1] It should be noted that the Greek American student organization at Queens College, where all of the interviewees are students, is titled the "Greek Orthodox Club." It sponsors weekly visits by a priest who hears the confessions of students and a priest is present during most public events in order to offer blessings and "spiritual leadership."

to the church during the holidays because of all the chanting, the robes the priests wear, the smell of the incense. You don't have to be very religious to like all these things."

Friends, Language, and Leisure

All of the respondents attended Greek parochial schools for all or most of their primary education. It was noted that this was extremely important for them, but they did not stress any school rituals and practices. They stressed the friendships they had formed and their continuing tendency to socialize only with other Greek Americans. "My friends from Greek school are like my brothers and sisters. We still hang out together and will always be close." The typical forms of leisure seem to be very limited and predictable. All noted that they go out with their friends at least twice a week. This either entails going to Greek coffee shops or, on the weekends, discos. A typical outing seems to be going to a cafe and drinking a *frappe* (iced instant coffee that is shaken so as to have a think foam on the top). Very rarely, it was noted, do they eat any desserts or have anything else other than coffee. When going to a disco, it was also very predictable in that it involved contemporary Greek pop music and quasitraditional Greek dances, especially the *tsiftetili* (also very popular with other cultures in Asia Minor, especially Turkish and Israeli). What was significant in this regard is the lack of any other forms of leisure: always going out with other Greek Americans, always drinking the same kind of coffee, always listening to the same kind of music and participating in the same kind of dancing.

When in Greece, all the interviewees noted that they felt much more American there than when they are in the United States. It was beyond doubt for all that they were much more comfortable and familiar with "American" culture than with "Greek" culture. Also universal was the inability to explain why this is the case. All the interviewees found it impossible to identify any specific reasons why they felt this way. Some noted that because they do not live in Greece they will feel less Greek than those who do but could not give any particular reasons why they would feel so different simply because they find themselves in a different country.

The Symbolic Order and the Mapping of the Greek American Everyday

All these practices noted above and found in the everyday lives of Greek Americans are experienced by those interviewed as pleasurable. Eating, going out with friends, attending religious ceremonies, dancing, displaying totems, and family life are all practices from which Greek Americans derive enjoyment. The practices in and of themselves, however, are meaningless in the absence of a symbolic mapping of them and their corresponding categorizations. What the interviews demonstrate, and what psychoanalytic theory consistently argues, is that only in relation to some "other" do the symbolic values of such practices become clear. In order to understand how individuals categorize everyday practices and identify what it is about these practices that they find to be enjoyable, questions must constantly be posed in terms of what it is about the ways that "others" enjoy that makes these other forms of enjoyment anomalous. In the case of the Greek Americans, the enjoyment of the Greeks in Greece constitutes one "other" in comparison to which we can identify what Greek American enjoyment is, and the enjoyment of WASP Americans tends to function as another privileged "other." It is false to assume that the "other" in the formation of the national identity is always to be found outside the territorial limits of the nation-state. German Jews represented a very significant "other" in the constitution of the German national identity in the 1930s. In the contemporary imagination of the United States, welfare recipients also function as a significant "other" best identified by their lack of self-discipline and aversion to work. So it is with the case of Greek Americans that WASPs function as an "other" when it comes to enjoyment. They do not care about their children, are money hungry, and, we could add, like to play golf and eat mayonnaise and sliced white bread that comes in plastic bags. In relation to these various "others" that appear in the sections above, we can deduce the symbolic order that categorizes and organizes all these everyday enjoyments of the Greek Americans.

The totemic displays to be found on the cars, clothing, and living rooms of Greek Americans seem to be the most general and clear expression of the enjoyment of identity in itself. This is a very characteristic American practice. Given the movement against the "melting pot" mentality and the rise of identity politics and multiculturalism, identity itself becomes a source of enjoyment and pride. This is a quality seldom found among Greeks in Greece, where the idea of multiculturalism, despite all efforts by the EU, is still not widely accepted, and, short of some major national sports victory, one would be hard-pressed to find a flag ever glued to a car or hanging from a balcony. The fact that Greek Americans gain enjoyment from placing Greek flags on their cars or wearing flag pins is an attribute that is a product of the contemporary American symbolic order. It is not particular to them, and most ethnic groups in the United States have similar habits: Irish, Italian, and Croatian flags can be found on automobiles throughout immigrant neighborhoods such as Queens.

In a very similar context, we see that the formal declaration of national subcategorizations becomes a key link in establishing the symbolic mapping of everyday practices. Those interviewed experienced socializing with their friends, and bonding with their fellow students in primary school, as Greek American practices because the contemporary American symbolic order tends to categorize people along ethnic lineage and origins. It is because those involved are considered "Greeks" that these close friendships appear as Greek American practices. The nature of friendship and comradery need not be any different from what is true of all other people; just the fact that the individuals involved and the schools and spaces where these friendships take form are labeled Greek American is sufficient for them to be experienced as practices that are "Greek American" in content.

Beyond these rather overt and easily discernable ways of categorizing and giving meaning to practices, we have all the other more nebulous practices that have already been identified, from the eating of oversized cheese pies to parents not charging rent to their children. Here we see some patterns in how Greek Americans categorize and map the libidinal practices that constitute them as part of the American national community. There is the tendency to experience and categorize those practices that are manifestations of the work ethic as very American. The willingness to work on the part of young Greek Americans, the tendency to work while going to school, and the fact that they strive to be economically independent from their parents are all experienced as "American" attributes. There is no question that this ensemble of practices is a great source of satisfaction for the Greek Americans and helps constitute them as part of the national community.

Similarly, all those practices that are understood as being manifestations of politeness and sociability are also experienced as "American" attributes. The requisite detachment when it comes to political discussions, being friendly toward strangers, not engaging in criminal behavior, and treating other individuals and cultures with respect are all seen as being characteristic of the Greek American community. In part, this stems from the idea that Americans are much more capable of deferring satisfaction. The Greeks are incapable of being polite and offering good service to their customers so as to secure more long-term business; they are out for the quick buck and detest having to serve others for money. Blacks and Hispanics also are less capable of deferring satisfaction and are much more likely to engage in criminal behaviors and other such "un-American" practices that illustrate this inability to properly defer pleasure. Since the Greek Americans are not so blinded by the desire for the quick buck and instant satisfaction, they are more open and friendly toward strangers. They see the long-term benefits to them as well as others in being polite and embracing multiculturalism. Family life also is a prime example of this ability to defer enjoyment, in that parents willingly sacrifice for the long-term benefit of their children and the children themselves will also sacrifice their own short-term enjoyment in order to work and contribute to the economic health of the family. In this way, the work ethic and the ability to defer pleasure function as complementary principles with which the symbolic order maps many of the everyday practices of the Greek Americans.

The emphasis on size and convenience when it comes to food is another organizing principle. Serving both as a metaphor for the "in-between" status of Greek American culture vis-à-vis Greek and Anglo-American culture and as a sign of the degree to which the Greek American everyday practices are structured by contemporary popular culture, the dual characteristics of size and speed are the principles through which food gains its "Greek American" character. Greek American food is thus similar to Greek food in terms of ingredients and taste but is very American in terms of its size and convenience. Similarly, Greek Americans derive enjoyment from "American" fast food in general, and this, as well, is experienced as an American attribute. In this way they feel a separation from the "authentic" Greeks given their presumed aversion to fast food and this serves as a link to other Americans because of their shared pleasures from fast food consumption. The Greek Americans may feel some guilt because of this desire for fast food and because of their distaste for many of the traditional Greek dishes, dishes that they think they should like and which they suspect are much healthier for them.[2] Nonetheless, the love of oversized cheese pies and gyros as well as greasy hamburgers is something, regardless of their ability to control the consumption of, that functions as an important "American" ritual and everyday practice.

The question of religion is an interesting one because, despite claims to the contrary, it seems to be viewed from a primarily religious point of view. The attendance of religious services on only the major holidays is viewed as being insufficient as a manifestation of true belief. Concurrently, the religious rituals themselves are viewed as being pleasurable, and the idea that god does not exist is seen as unthinkable (all stated that no Greeks are atheists because everyone must believe in some kind of god; those who claim to be atheists only do so to be controversial and create debate). Religiosity is in this way much more a component of the Greek American identity than it is the Greek identity. This not only conforms to the heavy presence of religiosity in American popular culture but also reflects the centrality of the neighborhood church to Greek American socialization. Traditionally, the only "public" space common to Greek Americans has been the church, and they are notoriously much more conservative and devout when it comes to religion than are Greeks in Greece. In this way, religiosity is viewed by the Greek Americans as a significant element in the constitution of their community and not simply some property of individuals or something that can be separated from the question of ethnicity.

Finally, we see that many examples of contemporary Greek popular culture are readily transplanted here. Thus, drinking Greek-style iced coffee and dancing modern Greek dances in Greek-style discos are common to Greek Americans in New York City. In part, this is also a hybrid of popular cultures. Certainly, going to night clubs and to sidewalk cafes is not alien to New York popular culture. The "Greek" character of these practices in this case is simply an articulation of practices that produce some levels of social distinction and exclusivity within contemporary American popular culture. These practices represent the most clear attempts at self-selection and constitution in that what is most attractive about them is their semblance of cultural authenticity and ethnic exclusivity. In this sense, it is not unlike the prevalence of golf playing and cigar smoking among many factions of the Anglo-American bourgeoisie. Through these libidinal practices, Greek Americans attempt to distinguish themselves

---

[2] It is often the case that Greek Americans have an aversion to traditional Greek dishes when they most differ from the standard foods found in the United States. For example, rabbits, pig jelly, buttermilk, goat heads, many soups made from intestines and organs, fish heads, snails, prickly pears, and okra are usually despised by Greek Americans, and they seldom eat them.

from other Americans through practices that are unique and culturally exclusive but eminently reconcilable with American popular cultural tendencies. Thus, cafes and discos are very functional for young Greek Americans in search of members of the opposite sex or for leisure activities that bring them into contact with other members of their community and function as a common point of reference for the whole community.

Interpellation and the National Political Community

We find that there is an entire ensemble of everyday practices that the Greek American interpellation is founded upon. Three basic types of everyday practices were identified: those practices that involve the totemic and habitual celebration of identity (displays of flags and so forth), those practices that are not celebrations of the identity but, rather, are everyday pleasures that come to be categorized and experienced as particular to a given identity (cheese pies and work routines), and those practices that are consciously instituted and practiced as a way of producing social distinctions and group cohesion (drinking iced coffees and dancing at "Greek" cafes and discos). It may be the case that those practices of the first type are central to the continued reproduction of identity, but they are also symptoms and manifestations of the interpellation itself. Only an already interpellated subject is able to gain satisfaction from flag waving. Moreover, the displacement of libido that takes place in this revelry of identity is itself likely only a stand-in for the broader ensemble of practices that function as the foundation of national enjoyment. This revelry of identity is thus, at least in large part, what in the previous chapter was identified as a pertinent effect, as something that only makes sense and can be explained as an outcome of interpellation and as a displacement of libidinal value to identity. The latter two categories of practices are much more fundamental in the interpellation of national individuals. These include a great number of everyday practices, from eating and drinking to working and socializing, that are of libidinal value and that come to be mapped and imbued with a national meaning by the symbolic order. Participation in these practices becomes the material foundation of the interpellation, and the enjoyment operant in these practices gives the identity its causal weight and social significance.

Some of these practices seem to gain their nationalist meaning through their incorporation into fundamental myths regarding the national character. Thus, some of the everyday practices identified as central in the Greek American interpellation gain their nationalist character by being incorporated into the myths of the American work ethic and the ability of Americans to defer their passions and pleasure seeking in order to secure their own long-term interests and for the communal good. Those practices of a more self-selective character that function to produce cultural distinctions and group cohesion among the national subgroups also display a strong nationalist function. By further ritualizing and formalizing the existence of national individuals as members of subgroups, the general status of these individuals as members of the national community is augmented and further cemented by the relatively homogenous practices and strong libidinal connections operant in their own immediate community. Thus, the coffee drinking and dancing of the Greek Americans, the golf playing and the cigar smoking of the corporate middle Americans, the football mania and barbeque traditions of Texans, and so forth, function as strong libidinal bonds to both the immediate cultural community as well as the more abstract and nebulous national political community in the sense that each subgroup reproduces and defends its proper symbolic and cultural space as its version of proper "American" life.

In all cases, practices and their libidinal content are paramount. To go back to Memmi, it is the real enjoyment operant in the everyday practices themselves that explains the tendency of well-intentioned colonialists to assume a racist stance toward the colonized. In the case of the Greek Americans, it is their participation in and repetition of a nebulous ensemble of everyday practices that constitutes them as national individuals and binds them in a libidinal way to the political community. Although discourse and the symbolic order are also very important variables and a necessary component of any attempt to explain the national political community, causal primacy lies with the practices that give weight and substance to the words and symbols. The ideas outlined in the previous chapter have been applied here in an attempt to illustrate the utility that this approach may have in regard to the question of the production of the national political community. This brief experiment in the empirical application of the materialist approach I have outlined demonstrates that it is possible to conduct empirical research by way of these ideas and that such empirical research contains a significant amount of analytical potential.

What the previous two chapters also demonstrate is that it is possible and desirable to produce a materialist explanation of the national political community. The idea that the nation is simply a symbolic construct or a genetic characteristic of all social formations can be countered by way of the materialist approach. The existence of the state itself is dependent upon the successful interpellation of individuals as national subjects, and the analytical requisites of understanding this process of nationalization demands that theoretical and empirical emphasis be placed on the everyday automations and repetitions that underpin these interpellations.

6

Tentative Conclusions and Notes Toward Future Study

Leonard Cohen as Political Theorist

With all the discussion of ideology and legitimation, it may appear that the preceding analysis has little to do with a large segment of topics typically associated with the state, those having to do with its oppressive and repressive functions—questions of violence, the police, surveillance, and so forth. After all, at a time when the state's means of coercion result in thousands if not millions of deaths each year, at a time when, roughly, one in ten black males in the United States is in prison, at a time when the United States routinely bombs and starves peoples around the world in the name of global order and human rights, at a time when the Chinese and Indian states have displaced millions in the name of modernization and development, and the list can go on and on, at this time, it may seem a bit frivolous to be discussing the historical and sociological niceties of the ontology of the state. The question of the production and reproduction of the state, however, is intimately tied to all its characteristics, including its violent and repressive ones.

In the song "A Singer Must Die," the poet/novelist/songwriter Leonard Cohen has perhaps best summarized the link between the question of the state's existence and its repressive functions. In a very startling verse, from the perspective of the arguments found here, Cohen writes, "and long live the state by whoever it's made." Cohen recognizes that the state is a product of society and, at the same time, that the who and how of its "making" are skewed and obscured. More interesting still is the context within which this line is found. "A Singer Must Die" centers on a singer who is sentenced to death "for the lie in his voice." Those responsible for this are largely acting against their will, the "judge has no choice," and the ladies who "go moist" do not desire this fate either. Nevertheless, everyone involved, from the singer who confesses to his crime to the judge and the observants, are all under a compulsion. It is this compulsion, this "probability to act" as Weber might put it, that is in question here. Cohen is illustrating the state's repressive moment as mainly not some violent terror from above but as a compulsion to do one's duty and show respect for the laws and public good. To say that the state is a social fact is not simply to say that it is caused by society but also that it is manifest as a coercive power over the individual. As Durkheim put it in his classic statement on what a social fact is:

Here, then, is a category of facts which present very special characteristics: they consist of manners of acting, thinking and feeling external to the individual, which are invested with a coercive power by virtue of which they exercise control over him. (Durkheim 1982, 52)

Cohen has gotten to the heart of the problem. The question of the state's repression is one of how our individual thinking and acting are determined and guided by "the state," a social fact that is man-made and that we continue to reproduce through our actions and cognitive categories. Repression and violence are not the same; there is plenty of repression even in the absence of physical violence, and, we could add, a necessary precondition to much of the violence that exists today is that the vast majority of individuals accept their own state-defined "duties" and act accordingly. From this perspective, what is striking is not how much but how little violence exists. What is striking is that the nine in ten black males who are not in jail do little to challenge the legal system, that the millions in China and India accept their displacement with so little resistance, that the many actively accept the domination of the few so peacefully.

Considerations on Everyday Life

The concept of everyday life has enabled the framing of the question of the state's existence in ways that avoid the theoretical impasses that have become part of contemporary social science. As for Lefebvre, the emphasis on the concept of everyday life is intended as a tool toward the overcoming of the fragmentation of social scientific analysis that has accompanied the increasing division of social science into various disciplines and specializations (cf. Lefebvre 1971, 21–42).[1] The need to understand "society" as a whole, as a unity, as a process, necessarily involves the circumvention of a great deal of conceptual baggage that is synonymous with the objects, concepts, and methods that come

---

[1] This methodological function of the concept of everyday life is concurrent to its more overt function as a referent to social practices that involve repetition and that here have been conceived of as the ritualized and concrete substance upon which all the fragments of modern social consciousness and ideas are founded. At times, within the preceding chapters, it has corresponded very closely to the most overt use of the term in this way by Lefebvre, as repetitions that occur within the modern matrix of twenty-four-hour segments—it is in this sense, for example, that Lefebvre discusses James Joyce's *Ulysses* as the first work of art that takes everyday life as its object (Lefebvre 1971, 1–11) and declares everyday life totally absent in a great many premodern societies (Lefebvre 1971, 29). At other times, it has corresponded simply to material social practices, irrespective of their ubiquity or exact temporal nature—it is in this more general sense that rituals of separation, for example, were considered as within everyday life, even though, for most of us, the practices involved in campaign finance and congressional gift-giving are likely foreign to our daily repetitions.

to distinguish the various disciplines within social science. To the degree that the state is a social fact and, as such, is manifest as a compulsion upon the minds and bodies of real people, its existence cannot be limited to the various bits of truth that may be visible through the fractured lenses of the competing disciplines and subdisciplines of social science.[2] A social compulsion must be understood in its totality, as a product of a totality of practices not limited by the typical academic boundaries and departmental subfields.

This emphasis on avoiding the fragmentation of analysis combined with the requisites of explaining the social existence of the state has had significant ramifications upon the epistemological tone of the present work as well as its exposition and conceptual movements. The need to avoid the fragmentation that tends to accompany the increased formal differentiation of social science also extends to the question of the means-ends relationship between theory and its object of analysis. The theoretical appropriations that have taken place in the preceding chapters have tended to be very strategic with the emphasis on explaining concrete social realities. The fragmentation of the social sciences has led to an increasing schism between "theory" and "empirical analysis" and, in turn, to increased scholasticism. The object of social scientific theory is not the interpretation of theoretical texts. Neither Plato's dialogues nor Kant's ethics are proper objects of theory. Theory is not its own end. Theory and the theoretical moment of intellectual production are only a means toward the explanation of the concrete. The typical rationalist epistemic movement that has been so fundamental to modern social inquiry, the movement from the abstract to the concrete, thus falls prey to the increasing fracturing of the modern academy. As the various pieces of social science become increasingly autonomous, they are more and more founded upon a tautology that is incomprehensible outside of that particular field. Bourdieu has noted that as social fields become more and more autonomous, they not only will tend to have their own laws but that their fundamental law tends to be a tautology: "That of the economic field, which has been elaborated by utilitarian philosophers, business is business; that of the artistic field, which has been posed explicitly by the so-called art for art's sake school; the end of art is art" (Bourdieu 1998, 83). So it increasingly becomes for political and social theory today as well as other academic fields, theory for the sake of theory, empiricist description for the sake of empiricist description, sta-

---

[2] It should be kept in mind that the divisions that are so ingrained within the academy today have much less to do with the requisites of intellectual production than they have to do with Taylorizing academic labor and standardizing curricula so as to increase the "efficiency" of higher education and decrease the power of faculty by making them much more interchangeable. That this is the main and desired purpose of specialization is clearly stated in the founding Taylorist analysis of academic labor by Morris Cooke (1910). See Veblen (1957) and Barrow (2001) for an analysis of this phenomenon.

tistical modeling for its own sake, and so on.[3] Everyday life, precisely because it is so large and beyond the typical fiefdoms that characterize the academy today, becomes a useful weapon for circumventing scholasticism and the tautological traps inherent to each academic field.

What Is the State?

A central outcome of the methodological and epistemological framing that the concept of everyday life allows is the definition of the state as a social fact. Without this conceptual move, no materialist explanation of the existence of the state is possible. Although it may seem elementary that the state, as with any social phenomenon, should be treated as a social fact, this has not been the case, as already indicated, with the vast majority of state theories.

By discussing the state as a social fact, the "state idea" as it has been examined here is not an academic concept, it is not something to be found in the writings of Easton or Dahl—it is something to be found in society. The "state idea" has referred to the contemporary propensity toward certain perceptions and categorizations that are logically and historically necessary for the idea of a "state" to be intelligible and compelling. Through logical deduction and by way of the comparison of the state to the *polis*, it has been argued that the state is distinct from previous political organizations and forms in two ways: in its spatial organization along national/territorial lines and in its division of society into the public and private. Neither of these things existed before the rise of the "modern state," and it is through these categorizations and their requisite materializations that the state gains its positive ontological status. Thus, *the state exists when people view themselves as members of a political community that is concurrent with the formal national territorial markers of what constitutes the "inside" and "outside" of society and when people view their society as divided into two registers, the public and private, with the political apparatuses belonging to the "public" side of this split as an abstract embodiment of the political community and its interests and will.*

This is less a definition than it is a summation of the social-historical specificity of the state form. As has been argued previously, it is not up to intellectuals to define the state because, at least as examined in the present work, it is a social fact and not an academic construct. Rwanda and Afghanistan, for example, may be states in the legal sense of the term or according to some academic definitions, but the absence of either the cohesion of the national political community or of the acceptance that society is divided into the public and private spheres with the public sphere being the neutral repository of the community interests and political will indicates that the state is lacking in a substantive sense. In this context, it is not that either case simply fails to comply with some

---

[3] Jessop illustrates this circularity when it comes to state theory: "It is no more necessary for a critique of state theories to ask whether the state exists than for a critique of various religious doctrines to question whether God exists" (Jessop 1990, 7).

definition but that the political realities and present conflicts and struggles demonstrate that the state project in both cases has failed to become hegemonic and compelling to a great many of the people who live there.[4]

Materialism, the Public/Private Split, and the National Individual

The question of the historical constitution of the state and the causal mechanisms of its continued reproduction can be divided into the two interdependent factors that make the idea of the state and its political realities compelling and legitimate—the cohesion of the national community and the split of society into the public and private. The preceding chapters have been focused on these two problems. But the explanations of each have been united not only in that they are subsets of a larger question/problem but also because of their common materialist content and reference to the practices of everyday life. As has been noted in the literature reviews, this is by no means the first time that either the rise of the public sphere or the formation of the national political community has been recognized as inherent and constitutive components of the state. It may be the case that the way they have been combined and framed here is new but concurrent with this combination, and framing is the common goal of explaining each as a product of everyday life. It is not only that everyday life has allowed us to frame the question of the state in ways that avoided scholasticism and partial explanations; the focus on everyday life has also provided the materialist thread that unites each section of the explanation of the state.

Sometimes implicitly and at other times explicitly, a goal throughout has been to counter the idealist tendency within social science where language and discourse are seen as historical agents or as causes sufficient in themselves to explain social phenomenon. More specifically, to the degree that the social existence of the state was seen as depending on perceptions, on how social agents tended to understand and categorize, causal explanations have been sought to explain how it is that such perceptions come about. In all cases, the material practices and rituals that underpin and structure national identification and the public/private split in the modern social consciousness have been sought. This is not to say that discourse and ideas are unimportant; from the discussion of the two bodies doctrine to the examination of how the symbolic order maps the terrain of modern national experiences, discourse has been treated as an important and necessary component of any explanation. Nonetheless, the examination of discourse is only part of causal analysis. It requires that we also

---

[4] It should be noted that the empirical determination that the state does or does not exist is not an absolute. There will always be segments of the population who either fail to identify with the national political community or who fail to accept the public/private division. The judgment that a state does or does not exist in a particular place and time is thus a question of the degree to which these factors are accepted by society and the degree to which the nonacceptance of these factors inhibits and precludes the exercise of state power.

take into account, first, the socioeconomic conditions that may help explain the content and timing of such discourse and, second, the everyday actions and rituals of concrete individuals that help explain why they accept or reject the content of the discourse. This goal is partly desired because of its methodological superiority in a general sense (in that it is a more complete and compelling understanding) but also because it refocuses the social scientific gaze not to the few individuals and intellectuals that propagate words and ideas but to the great masses and their agency. The materialist approach adopted here is a bottom-up approach as opposed to the idealist fixation on those at the top.

By identifying everyday life as both the source of our difficulties to come to terms with the state-idea as well the material foundation of its social existence, this work places its emphasis not on simply uncovering some "discursive" slight of hand by bureaucrats and other elites but on uncovering those practices and everyday rituals that constitute and make compelling the state-idea. That political theory has consistently failed to address this question in a rigorous way, it was argued, is a function of the blinding effects of our everyday lives and experiences. The state is so central to our own existence and we are so dependent upon its categories for our understandings of society that breaking with the ideology of the state becomes a rare and difficult intellectual task.

Having asserted that the existence of the state is as a social fact and that the ability to explain the state is, in this way, an important and necessary step for political theory and Marxism to overcome the ideological residue and prenotions that plague them, we proceeded to identify and explain how the state's existence is produced in everyday life. It was argued that the split of the social into the registers of the public and the private is founded upon the emergence of commodity exchange as part of everyday life. It is not simply that there is some logical or structural necessity and homology between the state form and the commodity form (as some segments of the Frankfurt School and Pashukanis may have argued).[5] The participation in the exchange of commodities founds the propensity to accept and believe in this duality of the private and public body because already present in the practice of commodity exchange is this split of bodies into concrete and abstract moments. Individuals already have acted out and participated in the doctrine of the two bodies during commodity exchange, and their acceptance of the corresponding political doctrine is historically and conceptually a product of the emergence of commodity exchange. Similarly, the

---

[5] Pashukanis (2001) argued that the state is a functional necessity for capitalism in that the legal character of the modern state is necessary for the proper functioning of the market. He also argued that the abstract nature of rights and legal subjects corresponds to the logic found within the circuit of capital. Although the arguments found in Chapter 2 are compatible with Pashukanis's arguments (and also the somewhat similar arguments of Polanyi, Gramsci, and Althusser), they are more focused on explaining how the rituals and experiences of commodity exchange create the propensity for individuals to believe in the fiction of the public sphere and the two bodies doctrine and are not focused on explaining the functional position of the state within the circuit of capital.

conceptual short circuits and legal fictions endemic to the public/private split, its fetishistic nature, also need to be mediated and regulated within the practices of the everyday. As was argued, the rise of the concept of political corruption and its corresponding regulatory practices does much to explain how certain practices and ways of acting are instituted so as to enable the continuing hegemony of the public-private split.

The emergence of the national political community was also examined, and it was argued that the propensity for individuals to be interpellated as national subjects is a product of their everyday practices. In opposition to most theories of nationalism, it was argued that for national identities to be properly explained, individual subjects could not be taken as a given but, rather, had to be explained as a product of the nationalization process. The Althusserian concept of interpellation was appropriated and augmented in order to help provide a conceptual foundation for understanding this relationship between material practices and identity/consciousness. The brief study of the Greek American interpellation demonstrated that such an approach is conducive to empirical research and emphasized the need for further empirical inquiry in order to identify those everyday practices that lead to the contemporary interpellation of national subjects.

Beyond the main arguments summarized above, many of the innovations within the foregoing chapters are potentially important in and of themselves. The situating of the two bodies doctrine within the broader socioeconomic conditions of the time helps explain why the "political fictions" that Kantorowicz found so peculiar came to be. It also demonstrates the large degree of convergence between works of intellectual history and works of political history (such as Elias's) on the question of the state's constitution. The recognition that there are two distinct notions of corruption is an original contribution to the corruption literature and demonstrates that the public/private split is peculiar to modern societies and that existing works on corruption have consistently misrecognized the deeper political implications of the contemporary meaning of political corruption. The appropriation of Douglas's work on purity and her concept of rituals of separation allow for the examination and interpretation of corruption laws as a part of state reproduction and class domination. The reworking of Althusser's concept of interpellation is the first to allow for its empirical application. Similarly, the extension of the concept of interpellation by way of Žižek and psychoanalysis not only allows for explaining identities but also allows us to plot and specify their differing political importance and causal weight. The arguments taken as a whole, however, are much more than the sum of their parts, and, from the perspective of the present work, it is now possible to identify how future explorations into the issues examined here can be refined and guided by way of the insights produced here.,

Reconsiderations, Clarifications, and Notes Toward Future Analyses

The success of this work can be measured in two ways. First, by way of how well all the analytical reframing and epistemological redirecting discussed so far succeed in transforming the state theory problematic so that it is able to avoid and overcome the reification of the state. Second, by way of how well it functions as a general analytical position that can guide future research into its substantive particulars. It is obviously impossible to know now how this work will be received and if it will have the effect of redirecting the state theory problematic. It is possible, though, to take stock of the substantive arguments that have been made and evaluate what is needed for their continued development and refinement.

The examinations into the everyday practices that underpin the public/private split and the national individual have produced unequal results. Most notably, it has been found that the practices associated with the public/private split are much more generalizable than those associated with the production of the national individual. The experience of commodity exchange was identified as a practice that is necessary although not sufficient for the emergence of the public/private split. If the arguments here are correct, it is expected that always and everywhere the public/private split will not be thinkable and certainly will not be acceptable to the masses if commodity exchange is not a common feature of everyday life. This argument should be tested further through more diverse and detailed works of political history. Political histories that trace the acceptance of the public/private division and measure it against the degree to which the market and commodity exchange had become common would serve to further support this argument and would also greatly add to our knowledge of how the acceptance of the public/private split has taken shape in different places and at different times.

To say that commodity exchange is necessary but not sufficient implies that there are additional practices that further reinforce the naturalness of the private/public division and which function to reproduce this component of the state idea. For, although the ideological content of commodity exchange can help us explain why it may be the case that the private/public division is believable to the masses in general, there are many contemporary social contradictions and inequalities that work against the believability of this political fiction. The rules and rituals associated with political corruption are a primary set of practices in this reproduction of the public/private split. Applying the concepts developed here toward further studies of political corruption would greatly further our knowledge of how these rules and rituals are constituted as part of the processes of social reproduction and class domination. Beyond the question of corruption, there are many other areas of social activity that could be examined in order to identify practices that help in the reproduction of the public/private split. It may likely be the case that the school day has been instituted in ways that play out this split and make it compelling to the student. It may likely be the case that rituals governing proper eating etiquette also reinforce and mirror this division. The same could be true for the working day, or military training, or the rituals associated with jury duty, and so forth.

The everyday practices identified here as associated with the public/private split, particularly commodity exchange, are expected to be present in all cases of the institution of the public/private split. When it comes to the question of the national individual, however, no particular practice was identified as necessary or ubiquitous. Indeed, Chapter 4, the main chapter on the national individual, does not discuss or identify any everyday practice as a cause of national identification. It is impossible to have such a generalizable set of everyday practices when it comes to identifications; each society will have its own ensemble of practices that their identity hinges upon. As noted, even within a society, there will not be anything like a homogeneity of everyday practices or a homogeneity of how particular practices are valued and experienced. We could say that, in general, the practices associated with eating, leisure, schooling, work, family life, and so on will be important but that is little more than a truism.

What has been provided in the two chapters on identity is the theoretical model for how national identification can be explained as a product of everyday life and an initial step toward an empirical case study that has provided us with a few categories that will help refine future empirical studies. The study of the Greek Americans was too limited and partial to be a conclusive or exhaustive examination of the specific everyday practices that function as the causes of this interpellation. Although it does provide an initial step toward explaining the Greek American interpellation, this is secondary to its main function of refining the categories and ideas developed in Chapter 4. This application of the approach toward explaining the national individual provided a foundation for categorizing everyday practices and their relation to the national interpellation. The interviews revealed three mutually exclusive types of practices: first, those that are the result of identification (flag waving and other such overt nationalist practices that make sense only if that person has already been interpellated as a national individual). Second, those that are self-selective and come to distinguish the cultural subcommunities within the broader political community (drinking Greek coffees, playing golf, dancing the polka, and so forth). And third, those practices that are ubiquitous and do not presuppose the national identity themselves but which come to gain a nationalist meaning because of the ways that they are incorporated into national myths or stereotypes (from politeness, working, and elements of family life becoming incorporated into the myth of the American work ethic to fast-food consumption being tied to the stereotype of the American fixation with size and excess).

The differences between these three categories of practices will greatly aid future empirical research. The overt nationalist practices are what was termed pertinent effects, an effect that could only come about because of the identification. These practices serve as and allow for a measure of the libidinal value that the identity has for the individual in question. Once this is mapped, in relation to other identities and their pertinent effects, it is then possible to examine the correlation between the libidinal value of that identity and the libidinal content of the practices that are identified as functioning as its cause. By examining those practices that are operant in the self-constitution and reproduction of cultural subgroups, we see how it is that concrete communities create their own version of "national" life, how membership within these concrete communities reinforces the membership of the individual within the more abstract and broader national political community, and how individuals actively participate in the reproduction of their identity. Finally, by examining how the more nebulous and ubiquitous everyday practices gain a nationalist content, the relations between the symbolic order and the everyday are made more clear, and the mechanisms that translate the enjoyment operant in these practices into a national enjoyment become more visible.

Many empirical studies are needed in order for us to have knowledge of the particular everyday practices that are operant in the production of national individuals today. But just because the empirical dimensions of this project are so broad does not mean that it is either impossible or undesirable to realize. The conclusion that the question of the political community is not one of collective action but one of individuation points to the broader theoretical and political significance of pursuing this line of research. The attempt at applying this approach demonstrated that the concept of interpellation, first articulated over thirty years ago, can indeed be used for empirical inquiry. It also helped refine the category of everyday life for use in future empirical case studies and underscores the importance of phenomenological examinations of everyday life for understanding how it is that individuals today come to be constituted as members of an abstract political community and become attached to their national identity in a strong libidinal way.

Future research into the particulars discussed above is necessary and desirable. Hopefully, the overall problematic outlined here and its conceptual and methodological contributions will serve as a point of departure for such future inquiry. At a minimum, this work has demonstrated that the existence of the state cannot be taken as a given or as a product of nature. Furthermore, it has also shown that the lack of questioning regarding the existence of the state has functioned as a limiting force upon state theory and social science as a whole. The demystification of the state as well as the continued progression of social science requires that we take the questions examined here seriously and deepen our critical grasp of how the categories used in the spontaneous understanding that people have of the world and their positions within it are constituted and made compelling. Just as the theory of the state cannot be separated from the history of its constitution and reproduction, the constitution and reproduction of the state cannot be separated from the material practices and cognitive categories that characterize our society. Marxist state theory has provided some brilliant and illuminating insights into the class nature and functions of the state. The realization of state theory's political and analytical goals lies in its continued materialist efforts to reveal the sources of bourgeois political domination and examine the social activities that constitute the active acceptance of this domination by the many who are subject to it.

Appendix

GIFTS

The House Gift Rule prohibits acceptance of any gift unless permitted by one of the exceptions stated in the rule. Gifts allowed by the exceptions include:

—Any gift (other than cash or cash equivalent) valued at less than $50; however, the cumulative value of gifts that can be accepted from any one source in a calendar year is less than $100,

—Gifts having a value of less than $10 do not count against the annual limit,

—"Buydowns" are not allowed (i.e., a gift valued at $55 cannot be accepted merely by paying $6)

—Gifts from relatives and gifts from other Members or employees

—Gifts based on personal friendship (but a gift over $250 in value may not be accepted unless a written determination is obtained from Standards Committee),

—Personal hospitality in a private home (except from a registered lobbyist),

—Free attendance at charity, political, or officially related "widely attended" events if offered by sponsor, and free attendance at receptions,

—Anything paid for by federal, state, or local government.

MEMBERS AND STAFF MAY NEVER SOLICIT A GIFT, OR ACCEPT A GIFT THAT IS LINKED TO ANY ACTION THEY HAVE TAKEN OR ARE BEING ASKED TO TAKE.

PRIVATELY SPONSORED TRAVEL

Private payment of necessary food, transportation, and lodging expenses may be accepted from a qualified private sponsor for travel to a meeting, speaking engagement, or fact-finding event in connection with official duties.

Limit on number of days at the expense of the trip sponsor:
—4 days, including travel time, for domestic travel.
—7 days, excluding travel time, for foreign travel.

Entertainment/recreational expenses may not be accepted except as gift rule allows.

Staff travel must be authorized in advance by the supervising Member.

A form disclosing the identity of the sponsor, the purpose and itinerary of the trip, and the expenses paid must be filed with the Clerk of the House within 30 days after return.

Within certain limits, may extend trip at own expense and on own time. May take spouse or child.

Time limits and reporting requirements do not apply to government-funded travel.

CAMPAIGN ACTIVITIES

No campaign activities in any congressional office or room.

No use of congressional office resources (including equipment, supplies, or files) for campaign purposes.

No solicitation of political contributions from or in any congressional office.

Don't accept any contribution that is linked to any official action, past or prospective.

Campaign funds may be used only for bona fide campaign or political purposes.

No personal use or borrowing of campaign funds, and no use for official House purposes.

No staff contributions for employing Member's campaign.

No staff outlays for employing Member's campaign (other than for campaign-related travel taking place on employee's own time), even if the employee is promptly reimbursed.

Staff may do campaign work on own time, provided that the work is done outside the congressional office; but no employee can be compelled to do campaign work.

COMMUNICATIONS TO GOVERNMENT AGENCIES

No preferential treatment for the Member's supporters, contributors or friends—treat all constituents fairly, and on the merits of their claims.

Avoid "ex parte" communications in cases before agencies or courts (i.e., off-the-record communications to the decision-maker that are made without prior notice to all parties).

Otherwise, Members have broad discretion in helping constituents: may make a status inquiry; urge prompt and fair consideration; ask for full and fair consideration consistent with applicable law and regulations; arrange appointments—or, where appropriate, express judgment, or ask for reconsideration of decision if it is unsupported by law.

Members and employees may not contact an agency on a matter in which they have a personal financial interest.

May not directly or indirectly threaten reprisal against any agency official, or promise favoritism or benefit.

Job recommendations to Federal agencies for regular civil service positions may include only statements that are based on personal knowledge of the applicant, or address the applicant's character (e.g., honesty, integrity) or residence (e.g., lives in district or state).

INVOLVEMENT WITH OUTSIDE ENTITIES

Avoid mixing of House and private resources.

A House office may not accept cash or in-kind services from any individual or private organization for the support of any of its activities.

A House office may not jointly sponsor a town meeting or other event with any private group.

Do not let outside organizations use a copy of official letterhead, or any terms or symbols that may indicate an official endorsement, such as any official seal, or the institutional names "House of Representatives" or "Congress of the United States."

Official mailing lists may be used only for franked mail; unofficial lists must be purchased for fair market value if not already available for public use.

Members and staff may solicit contributions for charitable organizations qualified under section 170(c) of the Internal Revenue Code, provided that no official resources are used, no official endorsement is implied, no direct personal benefit results for the soliciting Member or employee, and registered lobbyists are not targeted.

Prior written approval from the Committee is required for all other solicitations.

CONFLICTS OF INTEREST

Official position and confidential information may not be used for personal gain.

A Member must abstain from voting on a question only if the Member has a direct personal or pecuniary interest in the question.

Under criminal law, Members may not contract with the Federal Government except in limited circumstances relating mostly to agricultural matters.

Spouses and other family members have substantial discretion in employment and investments.

However —
Members and staff should not do any special favors for family members. Members may not hire family members in their congressional offices.

OUTSIDE EARNED INCOME LIMITATION & RESTRICTIONS

APPLY ONLY TO MEMBERS AND SENIOR STAFF

Outside Earned Income Limit for Calendar Year 2001—$21,765

NO paid professional services involving a fiduciary relationship, including law, real estate, or insurance sales, consulting or advising, or medicine.

NO affiliation for compensation with any firm that provides such professional services.

NO use of name by any firm that provides such professional services.

NO paid service as officer or board member of ANY organization.

NO paid teaching without prior written approval of the Ethics Committee.

NO advances on copyright royalties in book contracts; royalties may be accepted only if contract has been approved by Ethics Committee.

"Senior staff" in 2001 is anyone paid at an annual rate of $95,652 or more for over 90 days.

POST-EMPLOYMENT RESTRICTIONS

APPLY ONLY TO MEMBERS, OFFICERS AND "VERY SENIOR STAFF"

For ONE YEAR after leaving office:

—A Member may not communicate with or appear before a Member, officer, or employee of either House of Congress, or any Legislative Branch office, with intent to influence official action on behalf of anyone else.

—Very Senior Staff may not communicate with or appear before the individual's former employer or office with intent to influence official action on behalf of anyone else.

A Member, Officer, or Very Senior Staff Member:

—May not represent or advise a foreign government or a foreign political party.

—May represent oneself, a state or local government, or the U.S. Government as an official or employee of a government agency or entity.

"Very Senior Staff" in 2001, is anyone who was, in the one year prior to termination, paid at an annual rate of $108,825 or more for at least 60 days.

Violation of these prohibitions is a felony under 18 U.S.C. Section 207. Penalties include fine and/or imprisonment.

Bibliography

Abrams, Philip. 1988. "Notes on the Difficulty of Studying the State." *Journal of Historical Sociology* 1: 58–89.

Agamben, Giorgio. 1998. *Homo Sacer: Sovereign Power and Bare Life.* Stanford, CA: Stanford University Press.

Althusser, Louis. 1969. *For Marx.* London: Verso.

———. 1971. "Ideology and Ideological State Apparatuses." In *Lenin and Philosophy and Other Essays.* New York: Monthly Review Press.

———. 1982. *Montesquieu, Rousseau, Marx.* New York: Verso.

Anderson, Benedict. 1991. *Imagined Communities.* New York: Verso.

Arendt. Hannah. 1968. *The Origins of Totalitarianism,* San Diego: Harvest Books.

———. 1998. *The Human Condition.* Chicago: University of Chicago Press.

Aristotle. 1958. *The Politics of Aristotle.* London: Oxford University Press.

Bachelard, Gaston. 1984. *The New Scientific Spirit.* Boston: Beacon Press.

———. 1987. *The Psychoanalysis of Fire.* London: Quartet.

Balibar, Etienne. 1995. *The Philosophy of Marx.* London: Verso.

Balibar, Etienne, and Immanuel Wallerstein. 1991. *Race, Nation, Class.* London: Verso.

Barrow, Clyde. 1993. *Critical Theories of the State.* Madison: University of Wisconsin Press.

———. 2001. "What Is to Be Undone? Academic Efficiency and the Corporate Ideal in American Higher Education." *Found Object* 11: 149–179.

Bartelson, Jens. 1995. *A Genealogy of Sovereignty.* Cambridge, UK: Cambridge University Press.

———. 2001. *The Critique of the State.* Cambridge, UK: Cambridge University Press.

Benton, Ted. 1984. *The Rise and Fall of Structural Marxism.* New York: St. Martin's.

Bhabba, Homi. 1990. *Nation and Narration.* London: Routledge.

Billig, Michael. 1995. *Banal Nationalism.* London: Sage.

Block, Fred. 1987. *Revising State Theory.* Philadelphia: Temple University Press.

Bloom, Allen. 1968. *The Republic of Plato.* New York: Basic Books.

Bourdieu, Pierre. 1990. *The Logic of Practice.* Stanford, CA: Stanford University Press.

———. 1996. *The State Nobility.* Stanford, CA: Stanford University Press.

———. 1998. *Practical Reason.* Stanford, CA: Stanford University Press.

Bourdieu, Pierre, Jean-Claude Chamboredon, and Jean-Claude Passeron. 1991. *The Craft of Sociology.* Berlin: de Gruyter.

Braudel, Fernand. 1973. *Capitalism and Material Life, 1400–1800.* New York: Harper Colophon Books.

Bukharin, Nikolai. 1961. *Historical Materialism.* Ann Arbor: University of Michigan Press.

Butler, Judith. 1997. *The Psychic Life of Power.* Stanford, CA: Stanford University Press.

Canguilhem, Georges. 1991. *The Normal and the Pathological.* New York: Zone Books.

Carnoy, Martin. 1984. *The State and Political Theory.* Princeton, NJ: Princeton University Press.

Castoriadis, Cornelius. 1991. *Philosophy, Politics, Autonomy.* New York: Oxford University Press.

Clastres, Pierre. 1977. *Society against the State.* New York: Urizen Books.

Committee on Government. 1995. *Report 2.* Western Australia.

Committee on Standards of Official Conduct. 2000a. *In the Matter of Representative E. G. "Bud" Shuster.* Washington, DC: Government Printing Office.

———. 2000b. "Letter of October 4, 2000, to Bud Shuster." Washington, DC: Government Printing Office.

———. 2001. *Highlights of House Ethics Rules.* Washington, DC: Government Printing Office.

Cooke, Morris. 1910. *Academic and Industrial Efficiency.* Boston: Merrymount.

Coronil, Fernando. 1997. *The Magical State: Nature, Money, and Modernity in Venezuela.* Chicago: Chicago University Press.

Das, Veena, and Deborah Poole, eds. 2004. *Anthropology in the Margins of the State.* Santa Fe, NM: School of American Research Press.

Deleuze, Gilles, and Felix Guattari. 1987. *A Thousand Plateaus.* Minneapolis: University of Minnesota Press.

Deutsch, Karl. 1953. *Nationalism and Social Communication.* Boston: Technology Press.

Dolar, Mladen. 1993. "Beyond Interpellation." *Qui Parle* 6, no. 2: 73–96.

Douglas, Mary. 1966. *Purity and Danger.* London: Routledge.

Dumont, Louis. 1977. *From Mandeville to Marx.* Chicago: University of Chicago Press.

Durkheim, Emile. 1982. *The Rules of Sociological Method.* New York: The Free Press.

Easton, David. 1965. *A Systems Analysis of Political Life.* Chicago: University of Chicago Press.

Eisenstadt, S. N. 1963. *The Political Systems of Empires.* Glencoe, IL: The Free Press.

Elias, Norbert. 1978. *The History of Manners.* New York: Pantheon Books.

———. 1982. *Power and Civility.* New York: Pantheon Books.

Elliott, Gregory. 1987. *Althusser: The Detour of Theory.* New York: Verso.

Elster, Jon. 1983. *Explaining Technical Change*. Cambridge, UK: Cambridge University Press.

Evans, Dylan. 1996. *Dictionary of Lacanian Psychoanalysis*. London: Routledge.

Fink, Bruce. 1995. *The Lacanian Subject*. Princeton, NJ: Princeton University Press.

Foucault, Michel. 1979. *Discipline and Punish*. New York: Vintage Books.

Freud, Sigmund. 1960. *The Ego and the Id*. New York: W. W. Norton.

———. 1961. *Civilization and Its Discontents*. New York: W. W. Norton.

Friedrich, Carl. 1989. "Corruption Concepts in Historical Perspective." In *Political Corruption: A Handbook*, Arnold J. Heidenheimer, Michael Johnston, and Victor T. LeVine, eds. New Brunswick, NJ: Transaction.

Geuss, Raymond. 2001. *Public Good, Private Goods*. Princeton, NJ: Princeton University Press.

Giddens, Anthony. 1987. *The Nation-State and Violence*. Berkeley: University of California Press.

Gourgouris, Stathis. 1996. *Dream Nation: Enlightenment, Colonization, and the Institution of Modern Greece*. Stanford, CA: Stanford University Press.

Gramsci, Antonio. 1971. *Selections from the Prison Notebooks*. New York: International.

Gunnell, John. 1993. *The Descent of Political Theory*. Chicago: University of Chicago Press.

Habermas, Jürgen. 1991. *The Structural Transformation of the Public Sphere*. Cambridge: Massachusetts Institute of Technology Press.

Hansen, Thomas Blom, and Finn Stepputat, eds. 2001. *States of Imagination: Ethnographic Explorations of the Postcolonial State*. Durham, NC: Duke University Press.

Hardt, Michael, and Antonio Negri. 2000. *Empire*. Cambridge, MA: Harvard University Press.

Harney, Stefano. 2002. *State Work: Public Administration and Mass Intellectuality*. Durham, NC: Duke University Press.

Harvey, F. D. 1985. "Dona Ferentes: Some Aspects of Bribery in Greek Politics." *History of Political Thought* 6, no. 1–2: 76–117.

Heidenheimer, Arnold J., Michael Johnston, and Victor T. LeVine. 1989. "Terms, Concepts, and Definitions: An Introduction." In *Political Corruption: A Handbook*, Arnold J. Heidenheimer, Michael Johnston, and Victor T. LeVine, eds. New Brunswick, NJ: Transaction.

Held, David. 1989. *Political Theory and the Modern State*. Stanford, CA: Stanford University Press.

Herzfeld, Michael. 1992. *The Social Production of Indifference: Exploring the Symbolic Roots of Western Bureaucracy*. Chicago: University of Chicago Press.

Hirschman, Albert. 1977. *The Passions and the Interests*. Princeton, NJ: Princeton University Press.

Hirst, Paul. 1979. *On Law and Ideology*. Atlantic Highlands, NJ: Humanities Press.

Hobbes, Thomas. 1962. *Leviathan*. New York: Collier Books.

Hobsbawm, E. J. 1990. *Nations and Nationalism since 1780*. Cambridge, UK: Cambridge University Press

Huntington, Samuel. 1989. "Modernization and Corruption." In *Political Corruption: A Handbook*, Arnold J. Heidenheimer, Michael Johnston, and Victor T. LeVine, eds. New Brunswick, NJ: Transaction.

Hyppolite, Jean. 1969. *Studies on Marx and Hegel*. New York: Harper and Row.

Independent Commission against Corruption. 1992a. *Report on Investigation into the Metherell Resignation and Appointment*. New South Wales.

———. 1992b. *Second Report on Investigation into the Metherell Resignation and Appointment*. New South Wales.

Jameson, Fredric. 1988. *The Ideologies of Theory*, vol. 1. Minneapolis: University of Minnesota Press.

Jessop, Bob. 1985. *Nicos Poulantzas*. New York: St. Martin's.

———. 1990. *State Theory*. University Park: Pennsylvania State University Press.

———. 2001. "Bringing the State Back In (Yet Again): Reviews, Revisions, Rejections, and Redirections." *International Review of Sociology* 11, no. 2: 149–173.

Joseph, Gilbert M., and Daniel Nugent, eds. 1994. *Everyday Forms of State Formation: Revolution and the Negotiation of Rule in Modern Mexico*. Durham, NC: Duke University Press.

Kantorowicz, Ernst. 1957. *The King's Two Bodies*. Princeton, NJ: Princeton University Press.

Kelsen, Hans. 1945. *The General Theory of Law and the State*. New York: Russell and Russell.

Kosík, Karel. 1976. *Dialectics of the Concrete*. Dordrecht: D. Reidel.

Kouvelakis, Stathis. 2003. *Philosophy and Revolution: From Kant to Marx*. London: Verso.

Lacan, Jacques. 1981. *The Four Fundamental Concepts of Psychoanalysis*. New York: W. W. Norton.

———. 1992. *The Ethics of Psychoanalysis*. New York: W. W. Norton.

Laclau, Ernesto. 1977. *Politics and Ideology in Marxist Theory*. London: Verso.

Lefebvre, Henri. 1969. *The Explosion*. New York: Monthly Review Press.

———. 1971. *Everyday Life in the Modern World*. New Brunswick, NJ: Transaction.

———. 1991. *Critique of Everyday Life*, vol. 1. London: Verso.

Lefort, Claude. 1986. *The Political Forms of Modern Society*. Cambridge: Massachusetts Institute of Technology Press.

———. 1988. *Democracy and Political Theory*. Minneapolis: University of Minnesota Press.

Lenin, V. I. 1932. *State and Revolution*. New York: International.

Levi, Margaret. 1988. *Of Rule and Revenue*. Berkeley: University of California Press.

Lipset, Seymour Martin. 1963. *The First New Nation*. New York: Basic Books.

Lowith, Karl. 1993. *Max Weber and Karl Marx*. New York: Routledge.

Lukacs, Georg. 1968. *History and Class Consciousness*. Cambridge: Massachusetts Institute of Technology Press.

Machiavelli, Niccolo. 1962. *The Prince*. New York: Penguin.

———. 1970. *The Discourses*. New York: Penguin.

Macpherson, C. B. 1962. *The Political Theory of Possessive Individualism*. Oxford, UK: Oxford University Press.

Marx, Karl. 1906. *Capital,* vol. 1. New York: Modern Library.

———. 1970. *A Contribution to the Critique of Political Economy*. New York: International.

———. 1992. *Early Writings*. London: Penguin.

Mauss, Marcel. 1990. *The Gift*. New York: W. W. Norton.

Melossi, Dario. 1990. *The State of Social Control: A Sociological Study of Concepts of State and Social Control in the Making of Democracy*. Cambridge, UK: Polity.

Memmi, Albert. 1965. *The Colonizer and the Colonized*. Boston: Beacon Press.

Migdal, Joel. 2001. *State in Society*. Cambridge, UK: Cambridge University Press.

Miliband, Ralph. 1969. *The State in Capitalist Society*. New York: Basic Books.

Mitchell, Timothy. 1991. "The Limits of the State: Beyond Statist Approaches and Their Critics." *American Political Science Review* 85, no. 1: 77–96.

Mocnik, Rastko. 1993. "Ideology and Fantasy." In *The Althusserian Legacy*, E. Ann Kaplan and Michael Sprinker, eds. London: Verso.

Montag, Warren. 1996. "Beyond Force and Consent: Althusser, Spinoza, Hobbes." In *Postmodern Materialism*, Antonio Callari and David Ruccio, eds. Hanover, NH: Wesleyan University Press.

Negri, Antonio. 1991. *The Savage Anomaly*. Minneapolis: University of Minnesota Press.

Neocleous, Mark. 2003. *Imagining the State*. Berkshire, UK: Open University Press.

Noonan, John. 1984. *Bribes*. Cambridge, UK: Cambridge University Press.

Nye, Joseph. 1989. "Corruption and Political Development: A Cost-Benefit Analysis." In *Political Corruption: A Handbook*, Arnold J. Heidenheimer, Michael Johnston, and Victor T. LeVine, eds. New Brunswick, NJ: Transaction.

Offe, Claus. 1973. "Structural Problems of the Capitalist State." In *German Political Studies*, K. von Beyme, ed. London: Russell Sage.

Ollman, Bertell. 1971. *Alienation*. Cambridge, UK: Cambridge University Press.

Pascal, Blaise. 1995. *Pensées*. New York: Penguin.

Pashukanis, Evgeny. 2001. *The General Theory of Law and Marxism*. New Brunswick, NJ: Transaction.

Pêcheux, Michel. 1982. *Language, Semantics, and Ideology*. New York: St. Martin's.

Philp, Mark. 1997. "Defining Political Corruption." In *Political Corruption*, Paul Heywood, ed. Oxford, UK: Blackwell Publishers.

Poggi, Gianfranco. 1978. *The Development of the Modern State*. Stanford, CA: Stanford University Press.

Poggi, Gianfranco. 1990. *The State*. Stanford, CA: Stanford University Press.

Poulantzas, Nicos. 1966. "Vers une Théorie Marxiste." *Les Temps Modernes* 240: 1952–1982.

———. 1969. "The Problem of the Capitalist State." *New Left Review* 58: 67–78.

———. 1973. *Political Power and Social Classes*. London: New Left.

———. 1975. *Classes in Contemporary Capitalism*. London: New Left.

———. 1978. *State, Power, Socialism*. London: Verso.

Przeworski, Adam. 1985. *Capitalism and Social Democracy*. Cambridge, UK: Cambridge University Press.

Rogin, Michael. 1988. "The King's Two Bodies: Lincoln, Wilson, Nixon, and Presidential Self-Sacrifice." In *Ronald Reagan, the Movie*. Berkeley: University of California Press.

Shaw, Martin. 2000. *The Theory of the Global State*. Cambridge, UK: Cambridge University Press.

Shumer, Sara. 1979. "Machiavelli: Republican Politics and Its Corruption." *Political Theory* 7, no. 1: 5–34.

Skocpol, Theda. 1979. *States and Social Revolutions*. Cambridge, UK: Cambridge University Press.

Skocpol, Theda. 1985. "Bringing the State Back In." In *Bringing the State Back In*, Peter Evans, Dietrich Rueshemeyer, and Theda Skocpol, eds. Cambridge, UK: Cambridge University Press.

Smith, Mark J. 2000. *Rethinking State Theory*. London: Routledge.

Sohn-Rethel, Alfred. 1978. *Intellectual and Manual Labour*. Atlantic Highlands, NJ: Humanities Press.

Spinoza, Benedict de. 1955. *The Ethics*. New York: Dover.

Sprinker, Michael. 1987. *Imaginary Relations*. New York: Verso.

Steinmetz, George. 1999. *State/Culture: State-Formation after the Cultural Turn*. Ithaca, NY: Cornell University Press.

Stoljar, S. J. 1973. *Groups and Entities*. Canberra: Australian National University Press.

Strange, Susan. 1996. *The Retreat of the State*. Cambridge, UK: Cambridge University Press.

Strauss, Leo. 1978. *The City and Man*. Chicago: University of Chicago Press.

Taussig, Michael. 1997. *The Magic of the State*. New York: Routledge.

Therborn, Göran. 1976. *Science, Class, and Society*. London: New Left.

———. 1980. *The Ideology of Power and the Power of Ideology*. London: Verso.

Thomas, Paul. 1994. *Alien Politics: Marxist State Theory Retrieved.* New York: Routledge.

Thompson, E .P. 1967. "Time, Work-Discipline, and Industrial Capitalism." *Past and Present* 38: 56–96.

Tiles, Mary. 1984. *Bachelard: Science and Objectivity.* Cambridge, UK: Cambridge University Press.

Tilly, Charles, ed. 1975. *The Formation of National States in Western Europe.* Princeton, NJ: Princeton University Press.

van Klavern, Jacob. 1989. "Corruption: The Special Case of the United States." In *Political Corruption: A Handbook*, Arnold J. Heidenheimer, Michael Johnston, and Victor T. LeVine, eds. New Brunswick, NJ: Transaction.

Veblen, Thorstein. 1957. *Higher Education in America: A Memorandum on the Conduct of Universities by Businessmen.* New York: Sagamore.

Weber, Max. 1949. "'Objectivity' in Social Science and Social Policy." In *The Methodology of the Social Sciences*, E. Shils and H. Fink, eds. Glencoe, IL: The Free Press.

Weber, Max. 1958. "Politics as a Vocation." In *From Max Weber: Essays in Sociology*, H.H. Gerth and C. Wright Mills, eds. New York: Oxford University Press.

Weber, Max. 1968. *Economy and Society.* Guenther Roth and Claus Wittich, eds. Berkeley: University of California Press.

West, Cornell. 1994. *Race Matters.* New York: Vintage.

Žižek, Slavoj. 1989. *The Sublime Object of Ideology.* London: Verso.

———. 1991. *For They Know Not What They Do.* London: Verso.

———. 1993. *Tarrying With the Negative.* Durham, NC: Duke University Press.

———. 1994. *The Metastasis of Enjoyment.* London: Verso.

———. 1997. *The Plague of Fantasies.* London: Verso.

Index

About the Author

Peter Bratsis is a Research Fellow at the Center for the Study of Culture, Technology, and Work, City University of New York. He is coeditor with Stanley Aronowitz of *Paradigm Lost: State Theory Reconsidered* (University of Minnesota Press 2002).